Prai

THE GUMBO COALITION

"When Marc talks about building coalitions to successfully meet challenges, he's not only talking theory; he's sharing with readers what he's practiced his entire life."

—Tim Murphy,
General Counsel of Mastercard

"I found the words of *The Gumbo Coalition* ministering to my spirit. Readers of Marc Morial's blessed work will find an uplifting, challenging, and encouraging word they can use along their journeys to becoming their best selves."

—Bishop Paul S. Morton,
Pastor, Recording Artist, Author

"As witness and participant to Marc Morial's gumbo skills over many years, his actions speak loudly alongside his words. The combination wins the outcomes that are Marc's leadership hallmarks. To see him in action is to see his embrace of the youngest, least certain to the oldest, most experienced; to feel his strength building momentum tempered by his compassion for all, including those with differences; to witness his respect for each person in his presence and their desire to be encouraged and emboldened by his deeds and assurances. His story and leadership benefit us all."

—John Hofmeister,
Founding CEO of Citizens for Affordable Energy,
Former President of Shell Oil Company

"*The Gumbo Coalition* will help you avoid so many of the pitfalls I and others learned the hard way. Bravo Marc Morial, on penning this contemporary classic."

—Simon Leslie,
CEO of Ink, Author of *There Is No F in Sales*

"Marc Morial's *The Gumbo Coalition* underscores the essentiality of multicultural, coalition-focused leadership in the twenty-first century—a leadership where all communities sit at the table as equals."

—Janet Murguía,
President and CEO of UnidosUS

"Marc Morial is a star of strategy and execution. *The Gumbo Coalition*, a deeply personal, easy read, brings alive the generational wisdom that lives in the heart and soul of one of the most admired leaders of our time. A winning recipe for achievement, it illuminates behaviors that get in our way and demonstrates that you never have to sacrifice your soul to succeed in building on any front. This is a book that will help you thrive and save you time, money, and heartache. I wish I had it at the beginning my career."

—Susan L. Taylor,
Founder and CEO of National CARES Mentoring Movement, Editor-in-Chief Emerita of *Essence* magazine

THE GUMBO *Coalition*

MARC MORIAL

THE GUMBO *Coalition*

TEN LEADERSHIP LESSONS

That Help You Inspire, Unite, and Achieve

HarperCollins Leadership

An Imprint of HarperCollins

Published by HarperCollins Leadership, an imprint of HarperCollins Focus LLC, in association with One Street Books.

ISBN 978-1-4002-1629-1 (Ebook)
ISBN 978-1-4002-1628-4 (HC)
ISBN 978-1-4002-1631-4 (TP)

Library of Congress Control Number:
2019956839

Contents

Foreword

When my friend Marc told me that he was writing a book, I couldn't wait to read it. He's a lifelong crusader for civil rights, has had one of the all-time great careers, and is a gripping storyteller. I knew his book would be outstanding. Then I read it. I was right—it is outstanding. And it's outstanding in ways I didn't expect.

This book captures Marc's extraordinary journey from the youngest mayor in the history of New Orleans to the head of the National Urban League, one of the country's leading civil rights organizations. In these pages, he tells the story of that mayoral race, which he won against more experienced candidates; his fight to get racial bias out of judicial elections in Louisiana; his tough battles to reduce crime and police corruption in New Orleans; and how he transformed the National Urban League from a loose group of individual affiliates into a strong, united national team. Though this book does a good deal of looking back, it feels entirely current. So many of the issues Marc has taken on still demand our moral and political attention. So many of the fights he fought are still being waged by courageous activists across the country. Anyone who wants to know more about politics, organizing, and what it's really like inside the fight for equity—in New Orleans, in Louisiana, and across America—should read this book.

But while *The Gumbo Coalition* is a fascinating political memoir, it's also something more: a leadership manual, complete with checklists, tips, and pitfalls to avoid. Marc writes about how to increase your collective power by building consensus, how vital it is to communicate your vision to your team at every step, and how networking done right is about building purposeful and intentional relationships for the common good. This playbook is both practical and deeply principled. And the theme that unites it all—the core of Marc's leadership philosophy—is the value of building diverse and inclusive teams.

To my mind, that makes *The Gumbo Coalition* essential reading for people across sectors—especially business leaders.

The business case for diversity and inclusion is incontrovertible, yet too many companies either don't know it or don't completely buy it. C-suites are still overwhelmingly white and male. The pipeline numbers are moving far too slowly. Marc has worked hard to improve diversity in corporate America; he spends a chapter outlining how the National Urban League partnered with several corporations to set concrete goals to hire and promote more people of color. As he explains, there's a great deal of research that diverse companies, schools, and other organizations far outpace their competition in terms of profits, market share, innovation, and overall effectiveness. The top leaders of our time will be those who know how to take full advantage of America's incredible diversity—and who can build workplaces that make everyone feel included and valued. As someone who has spent a lot of time studying the corporate gender gap, I couldn't agree more with Marc's analysis—and I truly believe this book will help people embrace and activate their commitment to diversity, to the benefit of us all.

Marc describes his approach to leadership as gumbo, the classic Louisiana dish that melds African, Native American, French, and Spanish culinary traditions. "Throughout my life, I've found myself creating diverse teams before I even realized their power," he writes. "As I grew older, I realized that my penchant for coalition-building was really gumbo principles at work in the world."

I'm grateful that someone of Marc Morial's talent and character has dedicated his life to making our country more just and equal. He has made and witnessed history—and took notes all along the way. Now he's turned those notes into this wise and warm book. The country and our workplaces will be the better for it.

—Sheryl Sandberg, COO of Facebook

Acknowledgments

I want to generously thank my editor, Lavaille Lavette, who approached me in New Orleans at the 2018 Essence Festival and asked me if I had written a book. Lavaille both challenged and encouraged me to take on something that I've wanted to do for a long time. Without her guidance, energy, encouragement, and assistance, this project would not be where it is today.

Aswad Walker, whose invaluable research and assistance in wordsmithing and editing is deserving of gratitude.

Above all, the inspiration and support I received from my phenomenal wife, Michelle, and my three extraordinary children, Kemah, Mason, and Margeaux, were essential.

They laugh at my not-so-funny jokes, always support and encourage me, and collectively have served as a sustaining force through this process of many late evenings, nights, and weekends as this book project came together.

I also would not have been able to undertake this project without the motivation of my wonderful mother, Sybil Morial, my role model, mentor, and friend, who several years ago wrote her own book—a memoir, *Witness to Change*. Watching her labor with joy through the process helped push me to do something I've long wanted to do. And I owe great appreciation and support to the leaders and members of the National Urban League all across the nation, especially to Tina Pizzimenti and Cathy Ortiz, who assisted greatly in ensuring that my schedule allowed me to have sufficient time to work on this book against all of the demands.

I wish to thank all of my hardworking, passionate teammates and constituents who worked alongside me during my years as mayor of New Orleans. Their partnership, support, encouragement, and love have always been something I owe a great deal to.

Finally, I thank my late father, Dutch Morial, who departed this earth thirty years ago, for his ever-present inspiration and role modeling at an early age, as well as for the exposure he afforded me that has not only been a crucial component of all of the successes in my career but also undergirds many of the stories in this book.

Without doubt, there are many, many others who could be personally thanked, yet I offer my collective gratitude for all that they have meant to me throughout my life.

Enjoy and be inspired!

Introduction

I'm proud to call New Orleans my hometown. It's a colorful place known for Mardi Gras, the Essence Festival, and mouthwatering foods like crawfish, beignets, and my favorite—gumbo. When it comes to getting in the kitchen and whipping up a big pot of this Louisiana staple, I can hang with the best of them.

Gumbo, that dish you see on the menu at five-star restaurants around the world, was created in a time when things were tough in Louisiana. It was originally a meal put together out of desperation and necessity. When there wasn't enough of any one thing to make a meal, people would look in the ice box and grab a little bit of this and a little bit of that, then throw it all together in one giant pot. The result: gumbo, a simple, working-class, get-by meal that grew to be viewed as a five-star culinary masterpiece.

So, what does gumbo have to do with leadership?

A good gumbo depends on diversity and inclusion, the very thing companies, schools, and institutions of all kinds find themselves wrestling with. And by wrestling with, I mean most of them are getting their butts kicked, because their leaders have yet to figure out how to take full advantage of this nation's incredible diversity.

It's not impossible. There are leaders around the world who effortlessly foster diversity, inclusion, and coalition building. Time and again, their efforts result in increased profit margins and market share. Despite clear evidence of success, aspiring leaders have yet to grasp and internalize en masse what these successful, transformational leaders are doing. To put it simply, what they're doing is readily and consistently applying the principles inherent in the making of gumbo.

Gumbo was created out of the combined culinary practices of a number of cultures: African, Native American, French, and Spanish. Gumbo staples include onions, celery, green pepper, okra, chicken, shrimp, oysters—no matter what kind of gumbo you want to make, every one of those diverse ingredients and unique techniques are required to add the flavor and magic the dish requires. And you don't find this diversity only in gumbo.

Interestingly, the same skills the chef uses to make this delicacy are the same skills I use as a leader.

Creating gumbo as it relates to leadership is about building a coalition of unique ingredients or communities, each with unique skills, points of view, and flavors, each crucial in its own way. Creating gumbo requires the power and benefits of diversity.

When people talk about leadership, they say a leader has to be smart. But smarts alone without a solid plan and the ability to work well with others gets you only intellectually stimulating ideas with little or no productive action. Others say a leader must be able to plan, but what's a plan without the requisite knowledge and intellectual capital behind that plan? And again, how can a person implement a plan without being able to work with, inspire, and speak to the hearts and minds of the people involved? Even others emphasize a leader's ability to work well with others. But it doesn't matter how well someone works with others if they're lacking the requisite know-how and a solid plan that provides that know-how with meaningful direction.

Gumbo leaders rely on a combination of skills, abilities, and attributes. Not only are they intelligent and committed to lifelong learning and growth, they also possess the ability to envision, plan, manage, communicate, rebound from setbacks, and more. Being smart is not enough. Being able to communicate is important, but without vision, it's nothing. You must have a blend of these skills to be a transformational leader.

Throughout my life, I've found myself creating diverse teams before I even realized their power. As I grew older, I realized that my penchant for coalition building was really gumbo principles at work in the world.

When I ran for mayor of New Orleans in late 1993 and early 1994, I used intimate house gatherings, everything from public housing apartments to stately mansions to New Orleans shotgun houses, as my preferred method of meeting voters and allowing them to get to know me. At one of these gatherings, while thinking about what I was going to say, I noticed that the host had prepared gumbo. So I said, "Just like this gumbo is made up of different ingredients, so, too, is the city of New Orleans—different races, religions, neighborhoods, genders, and gender orientations, etc. And just like this gumbo that takes the best of every ingredient and puts it together, that's what my campaign was all about—bringing everybody to the table, using every individual's and every community's unique flavor to make one powerfully delicious dish." I was about building a true coalition of all New Orleanians—a Gumbo Coalition.

Just like the roux is the foundation of a gumbo, the African American community was the foundation of my Gumbo Coalition. To make gumbo, other ingredients are added to the roux. The same was true for my Gumbo Coalition. It was built to include not only African Americans but also whites, Latinos, Asians, straights, gays, young, old, and all religious groups of my marvelously diverse hometown, New Orleans.

Talk about lightening in a bottle! The phrase was picked up by my supporters and took on a life of its own. Soon, *Gumbo Coalition* became synonymous not only with my campaign but with the entire city. Note to self (and to you): always copyright your brilliance.

Somebody somewhere made a killing selling Gumbo Coalition paraphernalia, and it wasn't me.

Gumbo was also synonymous with my way of doing business. In every facet of my professional career, the Gumbo Coalition approach to leadership has served me well.

This book contains four sections, each highlighting different Gumbo Coalition lessons I have gathered from my forty-plus years as a leader. There are ten leadership lessons in all, and they provide a guide to help you achieve, inspire, and empower yourself and others.

Throughout the book, I will share insights through stories and life lessons. They contain the leadership tenets (gumbo principles) I used as a practicing attorney, member of the Louisiana state legislature, mayor of New Orleans, and ultimately as the current president of the National Urban League (NUL).

The openness to diversity and coalition building that allowed working-class cooks to make a gourmet meal out of scraps is the same leadership lesson that can make you the transformational leader you seek to become.

If you want to offer game-changing results for those you lead, keep reading. If you want the people and entities you lead to achieve inspired results, keep reading. And if you want to be the one who can take the things others view as "leftovers," be they people or ideas, and transform them into greatness personified, keep reading. *The Gumbo Coalition: Ten Leadership Lessons That Help You Inspire, Unite, and Achieve* has just what you need to satisfy your appetite for growth.

And who would have thought that all this wisdom could be found in a pot of gumbo?

Someone from New Orleans, of course. So, let's eat—I mean, read!

SECTION ONE

THE KID WHO WOULD BE MAYOR

Surreal is the only word I can use to describe what it felt like as I prepared to approach the podium as New Orleans' new mayor in May of 1994. That I was onstage, before the people of New Orleans at the Morial Convention Center, named after my father, former mayor Ernest Nathan "Dutch" Morial, who died unexpectedly five years earlier, wasn't lost on me.

In fact, surreal doesn't adequately describe the flood of emotions, sights, sounds, smells, and feel of the place, and the reflections that came with them.

In that moment, before addressing the thousands of attendees who were as much a part of that historic moment as I was, I reflected on the journey: that rigorous, contentious seven-month odyssey of a campaign that ultimately built up to this inaugural moment. I recalled that November day at the Fairmont Hotel when I officially announced my candidacy, surrounded by family, friends, and a packed ballroom of enthusiastic supporters. Though I was taking on one of America's most crime-ridden cities, during one of that city's most challenging seasons, those supporting me didn't think I had completely lost my mind to pursue one of the hardest jobs imaginable.

That diverse sea of people gathered around me, each from different walks of life and backgrounds, made up the Gumbo Coalition. Their diversity and dynamism made my victory possible, and I felt the presence of every one of them on that stage.

During our grueling campaign, however, not everyone was on my side.

The journey wasn't easy. I was initially labeled as an underdog candidate and was dismissed as someone who was too young and wet behind the ears for the big boy politics of the big city. With a crowded field of twelve mayoral hopefuls, I had to fight to emerge as one of the last two candidates standing. The runoff was hotly contested, and at times it felt as if I were running not only against my opponent but also against my age, my race, and my perceived inabilities from some combination thereof. There were detractors from all corners of the old guard New Orleans establishment that didn't want to see some "newcomer" take over city hall and shake up the status quo.

As I stood at the podium, I thought about the issues driving this run—the city's out-of-control crime rate and police corruption and how all the city's political, business, labor, and faith leaders, as well as the media outlets, wanted to know who had the best plan for addressing it.

The city's out-of-control crime rate was compounded by what I believed was corruption in the police department on a scale unimaginable.[1] New Orleans led the nation in the number of civil rights complaints against its police department as reported in various newspapers in 1993, including the local paper, the *Times-Picayune*. The corruption problem was so massive that two New Orleans police officers, Len Davis and

Antoinette Frank, are on death row today for committing murders of the citizens they were charged to protect. Len Davis ordered a hit on a woman named Kim Groves, who singled him out for being a brutal cop. She wasn't alone in recognizing Davis's reputation for brutality. By all accounts, he very much earned the nicknames "Robocop" and the "Desire terrorist." Davis was caught on an FBI wiretap as he ordered the hit on Groves; he was under FBI investigation at the time for serving as a lookout and guard in uniform for drug dealers who were trafficking in cocaine in southwest Louisiana.

Antoinette Frank was convicted of murdering her own partner, another New Orleans police officer, by one account after a dispute over a private duty detail at a Vietnamese restaurant. By another account, she committed a violent armed robbery at that restaurant that resulted not only in her partner's death but also in the killing of two members of the family who ran the establishment. Corruption extended even to the highest ranks of the department, with at least one NOPD deputy superintendent getting fired for close relationships with Mafia figures and lobbying the legislature on behalf of gambling interests in return for hundreds of thousands of dollars in fees.

During the campaign, the *Times-Picayune* endorsed my opponent yet vetted our plans to corral the city's crime problem and declared my safety plan overwhelmingly superior.

The bitterness and vitriol of the seven-month campaign didn't stop me from making promises. Hey, what kind of politician would I be if I didn't make a seemingly endless amount of promises? The kind who kept them all!

My thoughts were all over the place in those minutes on the inauguration stage before I addressed the crowd. And can you blame me? I mean, think about it. There I was, a New Orleans native son whose life up to that moment had been largely defined by, of all things, a ditch. Yes, you read correctly—a ditch. I had not been fed by a silver spoon and my life had not been shaped by a highfalutin lifestyle but rather by a long hole in the ground.

More specifically, I'm talking about the ditch that separated my predominantly black childhood neighborhood of Pontchartrain Park from the all-white Gentilly Woods, and how I spent my entire youthful existence and adult life literally and symbolically crossing that ditch.

I crossed that ditch to integrate elementary, middle, and high schools. I crossed it to become versed in the city's multiple worlds. I crossed it again to excel both as an athlete and honor student. And I crossed it again as lawyer and elected official, comfortable with crowds from the "streets to the suites."

It was as if my entire life of crossing that ditch, and operating in multiple worlds, had prepared me for that exact inaugural moment, that exact mayoral leadership challenge.

So there I stood, microphone and podium before me, the crowd eagerly awaiting a word from the one who had been dismissed as the upstart "Boy Wonder" by a group of veteran politicians I bested in the primaries, who viewed my victory as a wrench in their succession plans. I was about to share with the people of New Orleans my vision, my plans for eliminating that ditch and creating a truly unified city.

I was joined onstage by the New Orleans City Council, which comprised five new city council members in addition to two veteran members. Of the five new council members, four of them like me were under the age of forty and reflected the enthusiasm and youth our campaign had represented.

The new members had been elected on platforms that mirrored my own: a commitment to public safety, ending police corruption, and bringing economic development to communities in the city. I knew that, because of that alignment, we could get off to a good start.

As I stood at the mic, I reflected on the changing political environment in the nation, as well. Bill Clinton, a fellow southerner, was our nation's new commander in chief. And like me, he was considered relatively young for the office he was elected to assume. Also like me, Clinton readily committed to fully supporting an urban agenda, making him the first president to do so since another fellow southerner, Jimmy Carter, nearly twenty years earlier. I personally and vocally supported Clinton during his campaign and was full of optimism as he took office. But there were even more positive signs on the national horizon.

As I took office, I was joining an impressive community of mayors from Detroit, Dallas, San Francisco, Philadelphia, Denver, Minneapolis, Minnesota, Salt Lake City, Charleston, Chicago, Washington, DC, and Seattle. Each of them was similarly committed to the urban agenda coming from the Clinton White House, led by Department of Housing and Urban Development secretary and former mayor of San Antonio Henry Cisneros. Personally, I took this incoming class of elected officials as a tangible sign that my vision and agenda would have an ample array of talented, dedicated, strong, politically savvy, and fiercely committed collaborators and supporters.

Our campaign, via our Gumbo Coalition, had a vision to cross many of the "ditches" and dividing lines that kept communities around the country separate from one another. We were about tearing down walls and building bridges and opening doors. And the vision I was about to share with the city of my birth, the city I love, was going to speak to that. So I wanted to pack the house and make sure as many people as possible were on hand to hear it.

That's why I changed the inauguration to an evening event, making it less of a mayoral inauguration and more of a people's inauguration—a new beginning for a city too long held hostage by crime, ineptitude, a lack of leadership, and a defeatist attitude. Good people were accepting bad behavior in high places. The plans for progress they supported would inevitably fail.

When planning the event, we purposely tried to create a younger, hipper, more inclusive vibe. And I know from experience when folk over thirty-five attempt to make things more hip, it generally ends very badly. But I think even the cool kids in the place that evening would admit that we were successful.

This was thanks, in large part, to the many musical acts that participated. We had gospel, classical, and jazz. I was thrilled that my longtime, personal friend and jazz icon Wynton Marsalis so enthusiastically lent his once-in-a-generation talents to the proceedings. This was surpassed only by the presence of my mother, Sybil Haydel Morial, and my then twelve-year-old daughter, Kemah, as well other family members.

I chose the Honorable Judge Revius Ortique Jr. to perform the swearing in, making the event a family affair. Judge Ortique had been a close friend of my parents for more than fifty years and was a mentor to me. But Judge Ortique was so much more than family. He belonged to the state of Louisiana as a legendary civil rights activist who went on to become the first African American Justice of the Louisiana Supreme Court. This son of New Orleans and proud Dillard University graduate lent a level of historic gravitas to the occasion.

Moving the event to the evening merely added to the sensory overload I experienced. Six thousand people attended, making it the largest mayoral inauguration in New Orleans' history before or since.

The inauguration was preceded earlier in the day by the city's first Children's Mayoral Inauguration, where nearly thirty thousand K–12 young people were invited to the table to be full participants in the rebirth of their city. Why none of the mayors who followed me chose to duplicate that event still baffles me. There is not a year that goes by that I don't meet some grown man or woman who tells me how their presence at that 1994 Children's Inauguration changed the trajectory of their lives. This was the first visible display of my commitment to having a children's agenda. This agenda included our widely heralded and greatly expanded summer youth jobs program and summer camp program.

At the evening affair, standing before six thousand energetic supporters, the full weight of what was transpiring hit me. We had our work cut out for us. We wanted the longshoremen, teachers, hospital workers, and hotel workers who rarely had the opportunity to attend such events to be fully present and recognize their role in building a better New Orleans. It was important and symbolic that these blue-collar workers sit alongside the business and political leaders who attended these events regularly. It was also important that my words on that evening echo my campaign's call for a unified New Orleans that recognized we could do so much more together than we could apart.

I opened with words meant to show that this new generation of leadership, for which I stood at the helm, was not coming empty-handed. Rather, we had been groomed and polished by the individuals and times that came before us.

"The torch of leadership has been passed tonight to a new generation—a generation born during the baby boom of the 1950s, enlightened by the experiences of the 1960s and '70s, toughened by the hard economic times of the 1980s and energized by the hopes of the 1990s and twenty-first century."

I will never forget that I received by biggest applause of the night when I offered words to confront our city's biggest issue, crime, by restating a popular campaign line, saying, "We do face problems. We face drug pushers, gun-toting hoodlums, and thugs who prey on helpless citizens. We say to them,

'There's a new sheriff in town, and we are going to run you out of New Orleans.'"

Even though my tough-on-crime talk received the loudest outward endorsement, it was my words painting a picture of a unified New Orleans that earned the most profound internal affirmation.

"I want every child in this city, whether they live in Lakeview or Backatown, in Hollygrove or Gert Town, in Fisher or Desire, to have an opportunity to participate in a wholesome recreation program in his or her community."

I followed that up with a series of questions meant to get to the heart of the matter—the will of the people as had already been expressed in the election, seeking a brighter future for our city.

> This is a time of challenges and choices. We have important decisions to make. Can we rebuild our neighborhoods, revitalize our riverfront and our downtown business district, while preserving our historic buildings? Can we say that St. Claude Avenue and St. Bernard Avenue are equally as important as St. Charles Avenue? How will we spend our limited resources? Can we come together in new coalitions that care only for the pursuit of a better life and care nothing for the racial, class, and gender barriers of the past? Can we understand that we are in this struggle together—that no neighborhood can truly be safe until all neighborhoods are safe? If anyone is without opportunity, we are all without opportunity. Do we have the shared will to make our streets safe, to recognize that in some instances one strike is enough to take you out of the ball game if you violate our laws? Can we grasp the fact that our common goals are more important than any differences that we may have? . . . I will not be satisfied unless those opportunities are available to everyone. This is everybody's city—black, white, young, old, rich, poor, Hispanic, Asian, gay, and straight; Uptowner, Downtowner, Eastbanker, and Westbanker. It is our city to be shared equally by all.

I had campaigned to be New Orleans mayor as a thirty-five-year-old and was inaugurated at thirty-six—the youngest in city history. I was fully aware of the critics who viewed my youth and supposed inexperience as disabilities, not to mention those who believed that my race precluded any ability to meet the challenges of the office.

And there were many challenges. I would now lead the city with the highest murder rate in the entire United States (more than four hundred in 1993). According to the Federal Bureau of Investigation, New Orleans' nearly eighty homicides per hundred thousand people in 1993 far outpaced Detroit and Washington, DC. And in the first quarter of 1994, the homicide rate was up 36 percent over the previous spring.

Add to that countless other crimes, and the picture painted for the rest of the country was that New Orleans was one of the most dangerous places in the United States to live or visit (if you dared)—if not the most dangerous.

The reputation of local law enforcement did little to dissuade such a view. When I was sworn in, New Orleans held the dubious distinction of employing a police force with the most active FBI corruption complaints and investigations in the nation. That affected everything from the quality of education in the city to attracting new industry.

In spite of the statistics, I was overcome with a different kind of eagerness—an impatience to move beyond the pomp and circumstance and get to the real work. I had a plan for my first year in office that was painstakingly developed through a transition process that included the participation of over 1,000 citizen volunteers. These citizen volunteers developed an action plan for every department and agency of city government in a process that was widely heralded as a model mayoral transition initiative. As such, we had an action plan for everything from public safety, jobs, and housing to the city's mosquito control board. When it came to planning, we left no stone unturned, giving the team a new starting point to hit the ground running.

In the pages that follow, we outline how we began to implement one aspect of this plan: our approach to dealing with our city's retractable problems of violence and police corruption.

Most leaders come in with a plan for their first hundred days, and sure, I had that. But I was setting out to do so much more. I had a one-year plan because I was looking at the big picture and planning moves for the beginning of my second year in office predicated upon victories achieved in the first. Call me cocky if you want. I've been called worse. But only a one-year plan made sense to me given the magnitude of the problems the city faced in 1994.

For me, it was about always being prepared for the moment. And in that moment before giving inaugural remarks, I was beyond ready—mentally, emotionally, and spiritually—not only for the inauguration but to hit the ground running doing the daily work of being mayor.

SECTION ONE OF *THE GUMBO COALITION* HIGHLIGHTS THREE KEY LEADERSHIP LESSONS:

- "Speed Means Nothing without Direction"—A Leader Must Get Off to a Fast Start with a Solid Plan
- "A Wise Man Changes, a Fool Never"—A Leader Recognizes When to Modify the Plan
- "With One Canoe We Can Avoid the Waterfall"—A Leader Understands the Value of Building Consensus

Whether you're tasked with leading a corporate division, aspire to industry-wide leadership, head an international nonprofit organization, or serve as a key team member leading a major city, the first three of my ten leadership lessons will place you firmly on the path to success. So let's go.

CHAPTER 1

SPEED MEANS NOTHING WITHOUT DIRECTION

A LEADER MUST GET OFF TO A FAST START WITH A SOLID PLAN

Just a few days after the pageantry of the inauguration, reality hit.

The inauguration was on a Monday, only six days before the unfathomable 1994 death of nine-year-old James Darby, which haunts me to this very day. Darby represented the unbridled optimism New Orleans was capable of producing even amid the city's naysayers, who were always waiting for the sky to fall. He embodied the radical notion that, for whatever problems the city faced, certainly there must be solutions. A child living in inhumane conditions, Darby believed both he and his New Orleans neighbors deserved better. So he took action in a way reminiscent of the biblical youth David who refused to cower in the face of Goliath. Like David, James Darby boldly spoke truth to power—and expected those powers to respond.

Instead of a slingshot, Darby's weapon of choice was the pen, used to write a letter to then president Bill Clinton asking him to help stop the violence in New Orleans neighborhoods. "Dear Mr. Clinton," wrote Darby. "I want you to stop the killing in the city. I think somebody might kill me. I'm asking you nicely to stop it. I know you can do it."

Yet Darby's cry for help seemed to fall on deaf ears. Just nine days after his letter reached the White House, while walking home from a Mother's Day picnic, random gunfire took his life. Nationally, Darby and his voice became associated with the passage of Clinton's crime bill. For me, the Darby tragedy was a wake-up call to the importance of getting off to a fast start with a solid plan.

I'll never forget receiving that telephone call from my police chief informing me that this child, who just days before made national headlines, was shot in the head in an act of senseless gun violence. Beyond the jolt of anger and sadness that struck me, I remember thinking, *Okay, Marc, you're responsible for how the city handles this. You don't have the luxury of being an observer watching courtside anymore. You're on the court. In fact, you're captain of the team!*

For many, Darby's death signaled the victory of senseless, status quo crime that would dash any hope of change. My response had to be swift, bold, and unapologetically brazen. I couldn't allow the city to assume that Darby's murder, as well as the murder of so many other "Darbys," was simply the way things were.

And understand, crime in 1994 New Orleans had become accepted as part of the city's DNA. Even worse, the city's police force was so corrupt that both good cops and bad were viewed not as community servants but as protectors of a grossly broken system. I knew that if I were to be successful as New Orleans' mayor, I had to offer solid solutions—and do so immediately.

So we hit the ground running.

After years of watching well-intentioned leaders never make it out of the starting blocks for fear of rocking the boat, I knew a fast start was critically important. Many lacked clear vision or plans to bring that vision to life. I had seen so many new leaders fail to build momentum because they were stuck in minutiae—forever studying, researching, and analyzing yet never acting.

But I had embraced the value of a fast start paired with a solid plan long before I became mayor. Watching my boyhood idol and heavyweight champion of the world, Muhammad Ali, take on a competitor who would become his most bitter rival and respected opponent—Joe Frazier—ingrained this lesson in me.

Ali, "the Greatest," had been banned from boxing for roughly three years and stripped of his title for refusing to participate in the Vietnam War. His stand against that tragic war and stand against worldwide white supremacy made the boxing great a global hero and symbol for human rights.

With Ali sidelined, the fearsome southpaw Frazier emerged and won the world heavyweight title. Neither Ali nor the majority of boxing fans viewed Frazier's title as fully legitimate. Once Ali won his case against the US government and was reinstated, the "Fight of the Century" could take place in New York's Madison Square Garden, on March 8, 1971.

Ali had been known for his fast starts, which generally set the tone for an eventual victory. Fast starts were a big part of his game plans. But for whatever reason, Ali went with an uncharacteristically slow start, showboating and seemingly playing with Frazier. Frazier eventually won the fifteen-round bout.

Ali and Frazier would meet two more times in the ring, with Ali winning both fights. Frazier is still considered one of the greatest heavyweights in history, but I believe Frazier's victory in the first battle was made possible by Ali's inexplicable and uncharacteristic slow start—a lesson I took to heart.

For whatever mistakes I was bound to make as a new mayor, failing to get started fast, and with a solid plan, was not going to be one of them. There were four critical components to my fast start:

1. Have a plan.
2. Make sure your plan matches your vision.
3. Align the people and resources necessary for execution.

4. Overcommunicate your plan clearly and repetitively and to everyone involved.

COMBATTING CRIME IN NEW ORLEANS

My plan for attacking New Orleans' crime malaise was to shake the very foundations of every part of the city impacted by or responsible for crime. I wanted no doubt in the minds of New Orleanians that a new day had dawned—to clean up the police department and make the police trusted community partners once again and to provide young people access to opportunities that had blessed me so generously as a youth.

To do this, I had very bold specifics in mind. I had outlined my public safety plan throughout the campaign, debated it publicly often, and submitted the full plan to the *Times-Picayune*'s outside panel of experts. In a front page *Times-Picayune* story in early 1994, a few weeks before the March runoff election, that panel of experts declared my plan far and away superior to that of my opponents. In other words, the plan was tight and in place—at least, on paper. But executing it would take effort and time we did not have much of to waste.

The plan itself involved transferring two hundred police officers from highly coveted and cushy desk jobs and placing them back on the streets, both as a symbolic and very tangible show of force; setting a dusk-to-dawn youth curfew to remove young people out of harm's way; and transferring $1 million from the police overtime fund to the New Orleans Recreation Department to fund free summer day camps so that youth were not only saying no to crime but saying yes to positive activities.

For older teens, we brought together dollars from various federal sources to create the most expansive summer jobs program for teens in the city's history. It was important that our activities included activities for younger kids (the camps) and older teens for whom earning additional money was important and necessary.

Rather than supporting summer jobs programs at each public agency in the city, I brought them all together to create one single, unified jobs program. This program was to have a lottery system by which teens were chosen to participate. The reason for this was my purposeful effort to change the perception that these summer youth jobs were being filled through favoritism and cronyism. We made the selection process a grand and overtly public event, with local and national celebrities brought in to serve as the ones drawing the actual tickets to choose the jobs program participants. Again, this was done to emphasize as symbolically and tangibly as possible our move to an open and fair system that gave all the teens of the city who wanted a summer job a fair and equal shot at being chosen.

We were moving fast to provide city youth with the opportunities and support they needed, opportunities and support I enjoyed as a youth but which seemed to have disappeared over the years.

As we engaged in this work, we learned that speed means nothing without direction. In other words, a fast start without a solid plan is a disaster waiting to happen. After our team's diligent efforts, we had our plan, and it was rock solid. We were ready to get moving . . . almost.

Critical to the implementation of this plan was having all my handpicked people in place. I had an all-star team assembled. But I was still without the most critical person in our plan to corral crime, a police chief who shared my vision for the city of New Orleans and was ready to enact real, lasting change. Although I was committed to a fast start, I was just as committed to making the right decision about the new chief.

Knowing I would be tied to the hip with this person made the choice that much more pressure filled. I was resigned to rolling out my crime plan in stages, rather than all at once, as it made no sense to me to provide the complete plan when the city still lacked its new top cop. The city needed the crime plan announced and enacted immediately, even though my team was not yet at full strength.

Over the years, I have encountered far too many leaders who make the mistake of relying upon talent and instinct as a substitute for planning. I've also come across quite a few leaders so wedded to their specific plan that they were either unwilling or unable to make necessary adjustments. A detailed, well-thought-out plan is a must for a fast start. This applies to large companies down to the smallest, community-based nonprofits. But a plan's success can also depend upon the leader's willingness to be flexible and make necessary adjustments, both major and minor.

My all-star team worked late nights for a solid week discussing operational, fiscal, and political challenges. Together, as we sat around a large wooden conference table, we envisioned how our plan needed to be big. Our plan needed to be bold. Our plan needed to be impactful.

The all-star team that worked those long, late nights dined on Alexis Fried Chicken and takeout pizza, and in some cases worked until midnight and 1:00 a.m. after putting in a full day in the office. They were the most talented team New Orleans city government had ever seen. These were experts, but just as important, they shared my passion and zeal to make a difference in the lives of the city we loved.

Confident in the plan we created, I ignored convention and called a special session of the city council to make the first major announcements of my administration. Technically, protocol dictated that I alert the city council before calling a special session, but my gut told me that the power of this critical rollout would have been severely hampered had I stuck to protocol. I caught flack for the move, specifically from one member of the city council who said I was disrespectful.

Even without a new police chief chosen, I knew we needed to enact immediate change. I informed the police chief whom I inherited from the previous administration that I wanted to immediately transfer two hundred desk- and office-bound police officers and get them on the streets. I asked the chief a very simple question: "How long would it take to process these two hundred transfers?" When he responded "months" I knew two things. One, he was not going to be the police chief the city needed moving forward. Two, I would move ahead with this announcement and the order would go out on May 18—ten days after Darby's murder. We didn't have time to waste.

I demanded that the chief have whatever paperwork needed for approval placed on my desk immediately. Failure was not an option. Sometimes securing alignment calls for sweet talk. Other times it calls for strength.

But that wasn't the only bit of surprising news for the old police chief. The other aspects of my crime plan were just as audacious: setting a dusk-to-dawn youth curfew and transferring the $1 million from the police overtime fund to the recreation department for free summer camps.

Our summer jobs program, called the Mayor's Team, created thousands of job opportunities for kids.

Weeks before becoming mayor, I would regularly watch the late-night public access broadcasts of the city council meetings. During one meeting, police representatives were questioned about the amount of money the New Orleans Police Department had in its overtime fund. When the representative answered that there was no way they could spend all of those overtime funds, I made a mental note. That gave me the idea of where to find the money needed to bolster youth programs.

When I first suggested that idea, no one in the room thought such a bold move would be possible. Someone even joked about my audacity to even dare make such a proposal. But what they didn't know is the work I had put in by watching those city council meetings. I had everything I needed to make my case to both council members and police department leaders, thanks to the recorded comments about the overtime fund that were a matter of public record.

Speaking about coalitions, many leaders cling to "bootstrap" mythology—that success comes solely from intellect, power, and/or work ethic, with no help or support from others. That's a bunch of BS. That's the opposite of coalition building, the opposite of a successful strategy.

From my perspective, the most offensive words ever spoken are, "I'm self-made." There is not a human being past or present who became successful in any area of life without some support or involvement from someone else. In the fast pace of life, some people forget this. This individualistic, "bootstrap" mentality, however, convinces them that they don't need the help or support of others to be successful leaders.

However, my personal experience speaks to the efficacy of just the opposite. The truly great leaders whom I have encountered recognized early and often that they could not do whatever they attempted to do—introduce a new product, merge a new company into their existing operations, galvanize public opinion to support an initiative, or successfully grab market share from a top competitor—without the buy-in, support, talents, and contributions of countless others.

I knew full well that to successfully institute my all-encompassing public safety plan, I would need all hands on deck. I needed a coalition of support. Successfully transferring two hundred police officers, some of them kicking and screaming, required various levels of buy-in from both the police force and others.

This was critically important to me for some very personal reasons. When I was growing up, I held a job each summer from the time I was a fourteen-year-old middle schooler until I went off as a college student to the University of Pennsylvania. I didn't work at the Gap or the Footlocker in the mall, because there were no such positions available. In fact, there were no malls.

My jobs included a cornucopia of varied experiences, including pumping gas at a community Gulf gas station, moving furniture for a moving company, working at the daily newspaper (the *Times-Picayune*) in its mail room inserting advertising sections into the paper by use of an automated machine, working as a janitor, and working as a construction laborer after my first year in college.

These jobs, some of which were hard, demanding outdoor work, taught me the value of an honest day's work. They literally taught me the meaning of sweat equity. These summer jobs of mine also helped me appreciate the value of having my own money.

Moreover, these summer jobs provided me with all kinds of experiences and exposures and the chance to meet some of the most interesting people on the planet, some of whom went on to become my mentors. Knowing the value that summer jobs held for me personally, I believed passionately that providing jobs to young people as early as possible was as important to their overall development as classroom learning.

I was insistent on having a summer jobs program that included a kick-off orientation session on workplace expectations and a culminating picnic with awards presentations. We also opened many of the city's swimming pools after an emergency effort to repair them, some of which had been neglected for years.

This required buy-in from community, faith, and grassroots leaders. As a civil rights lawyer, I had to assure that the curfew would not be harsh or discriminatory. So, again, before any public announcement was made, we worked to win over forces critical to the plan's success.

The dusk-to-dawn curfew would not have been possible without ample community buy-in. Community members, in fact, were concerned that curfew violations would be treated as crimes and remain on young people's records. Accordingly, we promised that such offenses would not go on criminal records. We also decided to take curfew breakers to a central curfew center, which resembled a community center instead of jail. The goal was protecting youth, not incarcerating them—a goal made stronger by the input and buy-in of ordinary, everyday citizens. In fact, every aspect of our public safety plan required and was improved by the alignment of the people and resources necessary for success—the coalition we created.

Winning over the city council, however, would take much more finesse.

After the public announcement of the police transfers and other aspects of my crime plan, I spoke with both the press, the city council, and city leaders the next day. Essential to the effort was the work of two new community organizations: All Congregations Together (ACT), led by respected community organizer and Vietnam veteran Joe Givens, and the New Orleans Police Foundation, led by prominent business leader John Casbon. Essential to the work of building community support was ACT, a new, multiracial, multifaith-based organizing initiative. They represented the essence of the Gumbo Coalition.

The New Orleans Police Foundation came into existence to mobilize the leadership of the business community. This sprung from one of the key features of the public safety plan that we introduced during the campaign.

It was pure overcommunication, involving separate information sessions with the black and alternative press, the traditional press, business leaders, labor leaders, community leaders, faith leaders, and others. Again, the idea of the Gumbo Coalition, the power of bringing multiple ingredients to the table and melding them together into one irresistible delicacy, shined through. It paid off. Shortly after all those meetings, a citywide poll found that 85 percent of those polled were in full support.

As it happened, those numbers came out just days before the city council had to vote on the overall plan. Although one council member accused me of bullying them into a corner, in my eyes, I was providing them with a clear picture of what their constituents wanted and expected.

Needless to say, the public safety plan passed with a unanimous vote of the city council. The two hundred officers hit the streets immediately. Funds were now in place to provide New Orleans youth with the same kinds of opportunities I had grown accustomed to growing up in the Big Easy. And the youth curfew came to be respected and appreciated by city residents and national mayors looking to curb crime and increase public safety in their towns.

The curfew presented a special challenge we discussed in private. Here I was a civil rights lawyer and a former board member of the Louisiana American Civil Liberties Union (ACLU) proposing something that could easily be seen as restrictive and discriminatory.

A friend of mine, who was an ACLU member, told me he was thinking about challenging this in court. Hearing about this, my friend's better half told him that if he did that he would be put out of the house. Her response to opposition to the curfew I instituted seems over-the-top, but you've got to understand just how rampant and out of control crime had become in the city. People wanted to see something done about this problem—something fast, lasting, strong, and effective.

I'm proud to say that in the years we imposed the curfew, the city of New Orleans received no material complaints of police brutality or police misconduct regarding police interaction with curfew breakers. This was in large part because of the way the curfew was implemented and because we decided not to keep any records of youth who were returned to their parents. Curfew violators were brought to a curfew center we established, which was an old union hall owned by the city. Our sole aim of the curfew was to keep kids safe, not to place criminal rap sheets on them that would follow them for the rest of their days. As well, we enjoyed community support for the curfew because we made it reasonable. We built in exceptions for those going to and from work, and for minors accompanied by someone eighteen or older.

We were successful at getting off to a fast start with a solid plan. Fast-forward five years and our plan paid enormous dividends as violent crime had dropped by more than 50 percent, and New Orleans was heralded as a national leader in police reform, being recognized as an all-American city.

We replicated this approach on housing, infrastructure development, and government reform. For me, my long-standing relationship with the grassroots leaders—the roux of the Gumbo—was the linchpin of the development of broad-based support.

REUNITING THE NATIONAL URBAN LEAGUE

At the end of my second term as mayor I returned to the practice of law for about a year and then was honored with another transformational leadership opportunity. This time, it came in the form of president of the iconic civil rights organization the National Urban League. Growing up, city and state advocates of change were personal friends of my parents. Taking the reins of the National Urban League felt both natural and surreal—natural, as it seemed to fit me, but also surreal, given the institution's long and remarkable history of effective economic advocacy for black people.

Growing up in New Orleans, my parents had been active in the Civil Rights Movement. As a result, my siblings and I attended so many civil rights meetings, functions, and events that we qualified as preteen and adolescent members in good standing, which we were, as card-carrying members of the NAACP Youth Council. The impact was invaluable. When I was a preteen and teen, it was not uncommon for some of the country's most revered movers and shakers to come into contact with my family, mainly through our summer trips to the general convention of Alpha Phi Alpha Fraternity when my father was serving as general president. During these encounters, they discussed issues both big and small with my parents. Among the movers and shakers I met were Muhammad Ali and congressmen Ron Dellums and Charles Rangel. Other movers and shakers I met included Ralph Metcalf, a track star who was on the USA gold medal–winning relay team with Jesse Owens in Berlin in 1936, and Judge A. Leon Higginbotham Jr., the first black person appointed to the Federal Trade Commission, who later became a distinguished federal judge and was one of the most inspiring professors I had at the University of Pennsylvania.

At sixteen, I also had the honor of meeting Vernon Jordan, then the president of the National Urban League. My friends and I, including Tim Francis who would later become president of the Stevie Wonder Foundation, were in awe of Jordan, who was the epitome of cool in every way—well dressed, regal, self-assured, and deeply rooted in the history and culture of his people. Even more amazing, this civil rights and legal icon gladly and generously spent time chopping it up with me and my friends.

There were changes the Urban League needed to make if it was to regain its relevancy. And like 1994 New Orleans, the National Urban League of 2003 needed to make changes fast. But making changes quickly and getting off to a fast start with a solid plan are more challenging the larger and more complex the entity you seek to lead.

People often compare changes in large, multi-layered organizations to turning a ship. There is no "fast and furious" quick turnaround with large seagoing vessels. The turn typically takes so long to accomplish that the naked eye can scarcely detect the incremental changes in direction.

Yet turn quickly we had to.

When I assumed leadership of the National Urban League, not only was it an era when both many blacks and society in general questioned the relevance of civil rights organizations, but the organization itself lacked a clearly defined direction for carrying out its mission. The Urban League was present, strong, and stable, but it needed energy—a connection to an emerging generation of leaders and new ideas.

I did not have a crime wave to quell or institutional corruption to weed out, but the challenges were formidable, nonetheless. They demanded that I get off to a fast start and have a solid plan for the organization.

The work of the NUL is vast and impacts hundreds of thousands, if not millions, through its programs. As many of these programs have benefited local economies and the nation's fiscal health, the NUL has consistently received major grants from various entities within the federal government. Similar to my first days as mayor, I was faced with a surprise development upon taking over the Urban League.

Before I started the job, what was conveniently *not* shared with me was that the organization had just lost its largest grant—probably its most critical. The loss of those funds would impact staff salaries, operations, and programming. Frankly, I was pissed as hell. I also faced a major decision: Do I just walk away from the job, knowing full well I would be completely justified, or do I hold fast to my commitment as the organization's new leader and make some hard decisions?

Staying would mandate a particularly fast start. Staying would mean having to let some longtime NUL employees go. Staying would mean devising and implementing a plan to recapture those critical lost funds—a daunting task added to an already long list of daunting tasks.

Staying would mean owning the new financial state in which our organization now found itself, not publicly or privately pointing any fingers. Staying would mean accepting that, if I failed, there was a very real possibility I would not be around much longer.

I chose to stay.

I chose to get off to a fast start. And I had a solid plan.

The plan was to create one National Urban League with all affiliate chapters laser-focused on promoting the work, the brand, and the mission of the Urban League. The vision was of a national, nonprofit civil rights organization operating at top efficiency to meet its goals and objectives. The alignment of people and resources necessary for success involved restructuring the organization and its people while connecting with business, educational, political, and community-based entities aligned with NUL values. Communication of the plan involved targeted and effective messaging to employees and affiliates, national and local stakeholders, as well as the general public—the people we serve. I hit the road, visiting affiliates, doing TV interviews, visiting Capitol Hill, and reaching out to civil rights colleagues.

These fast-start priorities were achieved in many ways. I first established an open-door policy, encouraging any and all NUL employees to speak with me confidentially about their role within the organization, their perspective on the NUL's overall health, their vision for the future, or anything else on their minds. This helped me to get a 360-degree view of the NUL while also getting a firsthand feel for the established culture. I had used a similar "temperature check" of the mood and culture of city workers in New Orleans.

From there, I conducted a full-scale operational review and organizational assessment of the entire staff. I also visited NUL affiliates nationwide and held two roundtable summits with affiliate leaders, constantly gathering firsthand information. A fast start would have been impossible without first knowing what roles individuals played and whether those roles either complemented or conflicted with the overall mission and objectives of the NUL. The seeds of my overall plan were planted during this part of the process. From there, I was able to create an entirely new organizational chart complete with new job titles consistent with my vision for the institution.

As I prepared to preside over my first National Urban League conference in Pittsburgh, I was presented with a dilemma regarding my first speech. Should I present a vision-only speech or a more detailed plan-focused address? Those who advised me were of two different minds.

Some advisors said there was no way in six weeks on the job that I could devise a plan that would be effective. Hence, offering a detailed plan-focused address made little sense. Others were of the mind that a new leader gets only one chance at a first speech, so going for broke with either a big-picture, big-vision speech or a detailed plan speech was the way to go.

I chose my own route. I incorporated both my vision and my plan of action, which came in the form of my five-point agenda in a speech I called "It's Empowerment Time." My five-point address was to be a vision and plan all wrapped into one. Taking this approach was a bold move. It called for me to not only paint in broad strokes where I thought the National Urban League should go. It also called for me to provide detailed actions our historic civil rights organization needed to take to bring that vision to fruition, to move from idea to action.

I am forever grateful for the support system I had then and now, which consisted of Urban League executives and board members. The wisdom of these individuals was astounding in its bravery and astuteness. These informal advisors became critical as I stepped onto the national stage to lead an organization with long traditions and great challenges.

A five-point empowerment agenda I established was another critical component. This agenda focused on 1) education and youth empowerment, 2) economic empowerment, 3) health and quality of life empowerment, 4) civic engagement and leadership empowerment, and 5) civil rights and racial justice empowerment. It created a device for ongoing overcommunication of my vision and plans. It helped focus the attention of the national office and local affiliates on the same direction, working in concert with one another rather than in competition. The five-point empowerment agenda was a major element in efforts to rebrand the National Urban League. It's still used today.

Before I took over, the NUL had almost as many logos, color schemes, and taglines as a Mardi Gras parade. Each affiliate grew to become an entity unto itself. There was no cohesion. In fact, a noticeable level of animosity had grown between national office staff and local affiliates. I knew full well that, divided, this house would not stand. We reestablished one institutional logo, with one signature color scheme and one tagline to be used by all members nationally—The Urban League: Empowering Communities. Changing Lives.

Additionally, I established the organization's first Legislative Policy Conference, a vehicle that has afforded our organization a much stronger level of influence on national policies. Moreover, I shortened the annual national conference from seven days to four, a move that both saved money and made programming more efficient. We also established the Whitney M. Young Conference to provide professional development for experienced staff and volunteers and made the annual conference more outward looking. We revived and elevated the annual *State of Black America* report by adding a new statistical component, the "Equality Index," which measures social and economic disparities between blacks, whites, and Latinos.

Moreover, we borrowed and modified a business tool, the "Strategic Scorecard," and created the first ever National Urban League Strategic Scorecard to measure our performance and accomplishments annually.

In both instances, as mayor of New Orleans and as leader of the National Urban League, a fast start and a solid place was required, and it made all the difference in the world. Those fast starts created positive momentum that set the stage for more growth and victories that followed.

However, had I rushed in to start fast with plans of action that made no sense and were ill conceived or had no plan at all, the results for the city of my birth as well as for the organization I still proudly lead would have been tragic. But with a solid plan and the requisite sense of urgency, magic can and will happen.

In both instances, as mayor of New Orleans and as CEO of the National Urban League, I followed a careful script of planning with an aggressive fast start in execution combined with comprehensive efforts to communicate the plan to stakeholders. By the way, the grant that the National Urban League lost before I became president, I was able to recapture two years later through forceful advocacy and staff realignment.

GUMBO COALITION RECAP: THE PLAN

Moving fast without direction can be dangerous to your health and your bottom line. Whether you lead a business, school, or household, you need a plan. And that plan can't simply exist in your head. The plan must be in writing! Also, it needs to state goals and objectives; it must have a timeline; and it should apply inversion, which answers the questions "What do I want to accomplish?" and "Where do I want to be?"

How to Devise a Plan

Write it down—Your plan can't just exist in your mind or your imagination. It needs to be on paper, whether three pages, thirty pages, or more. In constructing your plan, it's important to include your team members. Some may elect to gather their team and devise a plan, while others may choose to hire a strategic-planning firm.

Listing Goals and Objectives—You need to be ambitious but realistic. Don't set yourself up for failure. You must think collaboratively.

Timeline—Here's how I set up my timeline. I identify the steps needed to reach my goal and break down my timeline on a week-to-week or month-to-month basis. In other words, I take the apple off the tree and I wash it before I bite it. My timeline identifies week one, two, three, and so on, so at any given time I can look and see where we are on our progression.

Inversion [Look-Back]—Inversion answers the questions "What do I want to accomplish?" and "Where do I want to be?" Here's how this process works for me. I envision how my plan is going to look at the end of the process, and then I work my way backwards to figure out what steps I need to take to accomplish my goal.

CHAPTER 2

A WISE MAN CHANGES, A FOOL NEVER

A LEADER RECOGNIZES WHEN TO MODIFY THE PLAN

When I became president of the National Urban League in 2003 I realized a change was in order, so I reached for my mayoral playbook seeking to do exactly what I did in New Orleans—put together, after completing an organizational assessment, an all-star team of top talent to lead the effort. Man, was I in for a rude awakening.

I hired a couple of executive search firms to find the best and brightest to fill key positions. My plan was to build an all-star team of top executives. Once hired, I expected this team brimming with championship pedigree to immediately get to work providing solutions to daunting problems. The plan was to create a win-win culture and chart a new direction for this mission-based organization. The reality, however, was totally different.

After the first eighteen months of housecleaning, reorganizing, and retooling, I reflected on the fact that I had made several changes to my executive leadership team and had also discovered some great talent in veteran Urban League employees. It was now time to meld the talent that was already there with new executives who would help continue our transformation.

Instead of coming together and getting busy handling the work of the NUL, these top-performing executives came together and got busy all right: busy bickering, backstabbing, and undercutting each other and even me. Astonishingly, for everything they possessed in aptitude, they lacked in attitude. And together, they meshed about as well as oil and water. In other words, they had zero chemistry. They became a living, breathing cancer to the well-being of the entire organization and the millions of people nationally that depended upon its programs and services. They were like bad gumbo. And if you're used to authentic, delicious Louisiana gumbo, when you get served some imitation mess—that is, some warmed-over soup masquerading as gumbo—it's not a pretty sight.

This fiasco taught me the importance of recognizing when a plan isn't working and needs to be modified. And boy, did this plan need modifying.

I also realized that a great team is not necessarily made up entirely of all-star players. Another way of saying that is, "The best talent doesn't automatically mean the best team," or, in sports terms, "An all-star team doesn't automatically mean a championship team."

As a huge basketball fan, the 1976–77 Philadelphia 76ers come to mind. In my opinion they were a team overflowing with talent, with the likes of George McGinnis, Darryl Dawkins, Doug Collins, Henry Bibby, World B. Free, and the legendary Julius "Dr. J." Erving. Considered by many to have the most talented roster in the NBA, they had an embarrassment of riches so deep, their second-stringers could have been a playoff team all by themselves. But those 76ers were unable to win a championship, even with a bench overrunning with superstars.

Now, I wasn't in their locker room, so I don't know the reason why that year's 76ers couldn't win it all. Maybe they didn't mesh and lacked chemistry. Maybe they bickered constantly. Maybe their egos were as big as their talent and got in the way of them fully embracing the team ethic. I don't know. But what I do know is Philadelphia never hoisted the NBA championship trophy until years later after most of the members of that 1976–77 roster were let go and replaced with new talent.

My National Urban League executive team for a brief period was like that 1976–77 Philadelphia team—all the talent in the world but no ability to deliver a championship. My executive team simply never meshed as a unit, fighting and infighting constantly. Their egos got in their way daily, and they never bought into that all-important attitude of cooperation and consensus.

I realized I had to swing the ax and fire this dysfunctional group to remove the cancer immediately. I had to modify my plan. And that's what you have to do when things aren't working out: move quickly or risk your entire operation becoming toxic. This happens when leaders don't lead. They see a problem, be it personnel-related or otherwise, and instead of acting to remove it, they wait around, letting toxic people or issues fester, hoping the problem will fix itself. News flash—it won't.

When you realize your initiative, your pet project, or your new hire isn't working or the plan isn't going according to plan, admit your mistake and correct it quickly.

In my case with my dysfunctional executive team, I confided in John Hofmeister, the chairman of the NUL board, about the problem and the action I wanted to take. Hofmeister, the chairman of Shell USA, was an executive coach and human resources expert by training whose private counsel and insight proved invaluable. He requested an executive summary of the situation, and once I provided it, he reviewed it and grasped where I was coming from. He was on board with my decision to terminate these executives. However, he warned me of blowback I would receive from some board members. When I went before the board, and they asked me why I was proposing such a drastic move, I simply told them, "I made a mistake by hiring show horses and not workhorses."

I have a long history of hiring successes. My batting average in this department is hall-of-fame level. This temporary setback was not the only time in my career when I had to make such an immediate and drastic modification to a plan. Since then, I have used leadership assessments in the hiring process to make sure I'm hiring folk I can work with. And the proof is in the gumbo. Once I swung the ax and cleaned house and put a new team in place, that new/modified group stayed together working magic for most of the last decade.

I tell leaders all the time, the hardest thing you're ever going to do is hire people. Let's be honest, when hiring you're always taking a chance. You can increase your odds of not making bad hires by performing due diligence, especially when hiring folk for leadership positions. But you're still taking a chance and will never be absolutely certain about a new hire until they've shown themselves worthy. As I said, my batting average is very high in making great hires, but this escapade was one of those instances when I didn't see around the corner.

The thing to remember is, if you make a mistake, change it. If your plan to go north is headed south, modify it and do it quickly. Don't let folk hang around thinking the problem will fix itself, especially if the problem involves top-level employees—you expect them to be team players and perform. If they are a train wreck, act fast. With employees at the developmental stage, you can have way more patience, but not with your top guns.

THE FREE AGENT WHO BECOMES A SUPERSTAR

Here's a very real example of a time I had to make a quick change from a previous course of action; a change that would have dramatic repercussions both immediate and lasting.

I committed as a mayoral candidate to find a new police chief through a national search. A major aspect of this commitment was forming a Gumbo Coalition national search committee for the right person for the job. I called upon trusted and reliable individuals to oversee this national search to identify the best choices from which I could select the city's next chief of police.

Members of this national search committee worked diligently for a couple of months and produced a list of ten names. Once they completed this task, and provided me with two additional names, it was on to the actual interviews. I did not want public pressure and opinion to come into play. Hence, I wanted to keep these names completely under wraps. Amazingly, we were successful in doing that.

Fearing press leaks, I rented a suite under an assumed name at the Hilton Hotel. Then, for twelve hours we interviewed twelve candidates, some from within the New Orleans Police Department along with several who were from outside the department.

After the interviews, I have to say, I was dejected and depressed. None of the candidates impressed me as the one who could lead the transformative project I envisioned, to make the bold move required if we were to be successful and flip the script on business as usual for those in New Orleans committed to criminal activities.

In a word, I felt stuck. Either I had to reinterview the twelve candidates, hoping and praying that one of them would reveal themselves as the shining star I needed in a way they hadn't revealed in the first interview, or I had to charge the search committee to start the process all over again.

This second option wasn't really an option at all. This choice of a new chief of police was critical to my top priority as mayor—drastically reducing crime and making New Orleans safe and livable once again. And the committee had been working for months. Everyone in the city was getting antsy over the decision that had yet to be made. Asking the search committee to commit additional months to this search made sense to me only because the ultimate decision on a new chief of police had to be a bull's-eye, winning choice. There was literally no room for error.

However, recognizing the critical importance of a fast start with a good plan demanded that something happen much quicker than if they were called to start from scratch.

While I contemplated which move to make, I just so happened to receive a call from a friend of mine who alerted me to the name Richard Pennington. Pennington had been a longtime police officer from the DC area who rose to become the second-ranked police officer in DC. For some reason, the decision makers in Cleveland's search for a new chief of police chose to pass over Pennington and go in a different direction.

I asked the person who called why Pennington didn't apply for the New Orleans job. It was surprisingly simple. He thought he had the Cleveland job in the bag. Satisfied with the answer, I contacted Pennington and invited him to New Orleans for an interview. Again, not wanting anything to leak out regarding this process and who was being considered, I asked Pennington to come to my office in plain clothes, wearing no police garb. In addition, I requested that once he arrived at city hall that he not identify himself as a police officer. I'm talking some real clandestine stuff here. The initial interview was just okay—mediocre. I recognized there was something there, something in him or about him that warranted giving him a second interview. But I was still on the fence about him being over the NOPD at this critical, do-or-die moment.

He shared with me his successes at reducing crime via community policing in Anacostia, a DC area I was very familiar with from my days as a student at Georgetown Law School. At this point I was intrigued, but far from sold. I informed him that he would have to come back to New Orleans, this time to meet with me; Marlin Gusman, our new chief administrative officer; Bob Tucker and Tony Mumphrey, co-directors of my transition team. This was outside the process. Some would say I had gone rogue. I found someone outside the search committee's list to consider for the job.

I was modifying my plan. Why? Because I didn't get the result I had hoped for, the result I and the city of New Orleans needed. This rogue move was by no means a criticism of the search committee. They provided for me the best possible options from their knowledge of individuals in play. They gave me the best of what they were working with. After that second meeting with Pennington I was still not completely sold, so I met with him again. If you're keeping count, that's three meetings, and still I didn't feel I had enough information or enough of a feel from him that he would or could be the person for the job.

Still not sold, I met with him a fourth time. For me, the fourth time was a charm. After that fourth conversation, I was confident that Richard Pennington was up to the task of leading the charge to remake the New Orleans Police Department and to make New Orleans' streets and communities safe once again. But now that I had finally come to a more than confident place with Pennington, this presented me with another dilemma as a leader.

Do I make this decision outside the search committee process or do I drag this along even longer, knowing I've already found the city's knight in shining armor? I pondered whether I should insert Pennington into the committee's search process or hire him on my own. I decided to hire. Why such a rogue move? Because, quite simply, he was the best choice. Also, as stated, local leaders on all levels were very antsy. The search committee had put in months on top of overtime months, and still there was no chief. The press made the absence of a decision a story of great concern. Our administration's bank account of goodwill was close to being in the red.

So I decided to roll out Pennington as New Orleans' new chief of police. I chose to do so in unusual fashion, however. I made arrangements to get him an NOPD uniform before he was even officially announced as the new chief. I also set up two rooms at Gallier Hall, New Orleans' historic old city hall. In one room, I invited members of the national search committee. In another, I had members of New Orleans' city council. Additionally, downstairs, I had the media awaiting a press conference.

From there, I walked into the room containing the national search committee. With me, walking by my side, was the six-foot five-inch Richard Pennington in a fresh New Orleans chief of police uniform. I then addressed the committee by saying, "Ladies and gentlemen, this is our new chief of police." I then apologized to them for veering from the process and explained the very unusual set of circumstances that demanded that I take the rogue course of action that I did. Afterwards, I thanked them for their work but reiterated that I made the decision I thought was best for the city and citizens of New Orleans. Dramatic, I know.

Then Pennington and I walked into the room with members of the city council and proceeded to give the same presentation. To be honest, the city council members were in awe. On one level, they were in awe that a new, young mayor would have the balls to make such a baller move. On another level, they were stupefied to the point of silence when they realized I had run this entire process and found the candidate with absolutely nothing leaking out.

After basking in the afterglow of the city council's amazement, we proceeded downstairs with the press waiting for the surprise announcement. They, like the search committee and the city council members, had no idea what was about to happen. But they knew it was big when they saw the imposing figure of Pennington march in, back straight, gaze confident, and dressed to the nines in his brand-spanking-new uniform.

I moved swiftly to the podium and proudly announced Richard Pennington as New Orleans' new chief of police. Then, without missing a beat or taking any questions, I whipped out a bible and swore him in on the spot. Talk about baller moves.

Even with a national search that included the best consultant in the country, I ended up picking our new chief myself, in a sense, with my own personal search committee. Just as amazingly, Pennington went on to become the city's best chief of police and my partner in overseeing and implementing my safety plan. That people came to discover that he had over three decades of service wearing the badge with honor and distinction, and that he held a master's degree, only added to his legend. Not only am I proud of the incredible job he did as chief of police, I am equally proud that, over my eight years as mayor, Chief of Police Richard Pennington was my only police chief. He later went on to serve with distinction as Atlanta's police chief, and has since passed away.

Was veering from my original plan needed? Yes. Was it worth it? Without any doubt whatsoever. Was it a risky move? Sure. Would I do it again? In a split second.

Beyond acting fast, how did I modify my plans to remove ineffective leaders as I did at the National Urban League? For starters I engaged in more direct hiring. I realized somewhere along the way that some search firms often recycle fired executives (or some forced to take a retirement package to avoid being officially canned). I still use search firms from time to time, but I learned to trust my gut and do more direct hiring.

I also interview candidates as many as four times. Why? Because anyone can provide a great interview once or twice in their lives, or inconsistently. I'm looking for consistency, and those three to four interviews allow me to see which candidates are great one day and flat the next, and which ones are consistently good.

This fiasco also reminded me of the importance of networking. Had I not engaged in lifelong networking, I would have lacked the connections to modify my all-star plan as quickly as I did. For some of my new hires to replace the bad Dream Team came out of my personal networking pool. I'll explore this topic of networking more in a later chapter.

CHANGE COMES TO LOUISIANA'S HIGHEST COURT

As Urban League president, I was a seasoned leader when I faced the challenge of modifying my plan to build my leadership team.

However, far earlier in my professional career, I faced an even more daunting challenge regarding whether to modify or not. That was the question I faced as a young, wet-behind-the-ears lawyer regarding voting rights and judicial diversity.

So, here's the situation. As a young lawyer returning to Louisiana fresh from graduating from Georgetown University's law school, I noticed immediately the lack of black judges in New Orleans. I was attuned to this reality in part because, while in DC, I was part of the law school's legal clinic. As such, I was exposed to the city's numerous black judges. But when I came back to Louisiana, the lack of black judges stood out like a glaring eyesore.

I looked around and asked, "Where are the black judges?" I started taking inventory of all judge seats in the city and counted roughly fifty. Of those, there were only one or two blacks serving on the judiciary. At the city's criminal court level, there were zero, even though 75 to 80 percent of the people who came before criminal court judges were black. So I asked questions and did some research. I found that the districts were literally rigged to not elect black judges.

I discovered there had been no more than a handful of black judges in Louisiana history, even though the population was one-third black. And all those judges were elected, not appointed. I realized that with blacks making up roughly 33 percent of the state's population, it should have been statistically impossible to have no black representation on the state's supreme court, not to mention a mere handful statewide.

My experiences growing up the son of civil rights activists would not allow me to sit idly by and do nothing about this political and legal inequity. In the midst of this reflection, a group of brash, young lawyers and I decided to challenge this system.

We put a plan in place. The ultimate goal of that plan was adding an additional State Supreme Court seat that would essentially be a black judge's seat. To do this, our plan involved filing a lawsuit against the state challenging its lack of adherence to the Voting

Rights Act in how the district lines for the Louisiana Supreme Court were drawn. That lawsuit became *Chisom v. Edwards*, filed in the US District Court for the Eastern District of Louisiana, with team member Ron Chisom, a community activist and civil rights legend, serving as the lead plaintiff. I was listed as one of the plaintiffs as well.

Chisom was not the only big gun we had on our side. We also had the nation's premier civil rights law firm, the NAACP Legal Defense Fund, collaborating with us.

For those of you who are not aware, the NAACP Legal Defense Fund was the institution created and founded by Charles Hamilton Houston and Thurgood Marshall. Marshall's legendary arguments before the US Supreme Court were made as leader of this entity.

In 1985, knowing we wanted to bring a lawsuit against the state over Louisiana Supreme Court district lines, we called Julius Chambers, a distinguished North Carolina lawyer and later a university president who was the leader of the NAACP Legal Defense Fund (LDF). He agreed to support us. Five years earlier, the LDF had successfully come in and challenged the gerrymandered lines that prevented the election of an African American congressman from New Orleans.

Finally, in 1991, after more than six years, the big day had arrived when the Chisom case was to be argued in front of the US Supreme Court. When we arrived in the nation's capital, we purposely chose to stay at the Howard Inn, a black-owned hotel.

We were arguing before the Supreme Court on the narrow issues as to whether the 1965 Voting Rights Act applied to Louisiana's judicial elections. The state of Louisiana had successfully argued in the lower court that the 1965 Voting Rights Act did not apply to judicial elections. The Supreme Court was our last chance. If we convinced the court that the Voting Rights Act of 1965 applied to the state's judicial elections, our case would then return to the lower courts and be tried on its full merits, and we would have the opportunity to show that the lines were discriminatory and unfair. If we lost at the Supreme Court, our case, even after six long years of blood, sweat, and tears, would for all intents and purposes be dead.

Once it was time for the case, we had the most satisfying pleasure of watching Pam Karlan of the NAACP Legal Defense Fund demolish her opposing attorney, who represented the state. By any and all measures, Karlan was brilliant, and I'm describing her personhood and her performance in court. She was a Yale lawyer and a former clerk for Justice Harry Blackmun. When she walked into the high court, she displayed her brilliance in its fullness and wiped the floor with her opposing counsel.

As we walked out of the Supreme Court, we smelled victory. When we got word of the ruling, we were not surprised. But we were still elated. We ended up winning in a 6–3 decision.

Without the NAACP Legal Defense Fund, our efforts would have been dead in the water before they began. Moreover, we had a team of the best "new generation" civil rights lawyers as local counsel: Bill Quigley, Ron Wilson, Roy Rodney, Walter Willard, Marie Bookman, and me. Bookman, Willard, and I decided to join *Chisom* as plaintiffs. But even with such support, many older, black lawyers counseled us against suing the state, saying it was professional suicide. We proceeded anyway and lost at the federal district and appellate levels. But recognizing a loss at this level was possible, we were not deterred. Our plan involved taking the case all the way to the US Supreme Court, which we did. And we won.

This was no quick process but a protracted fight. Along the way, I ran for US Congress in 1990 and lost and ran for the Louisiana State Senate one year later and won, the same year we won our Supreme Court case.

At this point, all the original naysayers who warned us against suing the state lauded us for our legal and political bravery. But our team realized the fight was far from over.

After the high court victory, we still had to retry the case at the district level because the Supreme Court had simply decided that the Voting Rights Act applied to judicial elections. And it was during this time that something outside of our control happened. Supreme Court justice and civil rights icon Thurgood Marshall retired and was replaced by Clarence Thomas—in my opinion, no supporter of voting rights. Moreover, George H.W. Bush (Bush 41) at that point appeared to be headed for an easy re-election that would give him, in all likelihood, another appointment on the US Supreme Court.

Members of our team, fresh off our Supreme Court victory, were ready to plow ahead, fighting in court for that additional State Supreme Court seat. I, on the other hand, recognizing the seismic shift in our situation with Justice Marshall now gone, believed it was critical that we modify our plan.

Originally a hardliner for fighting the entire battle out in court, I now strongly suggested that we seek a settlement. Initially, our team didn't like that shift in plans at all. I knew, however, that without Marshall's vote and if we returned to the Supreme Court with an additional Bush appointee, we could lose everything and have to put off even attempting to gain that additional seat for another generation.

But I was convinced that only a modified plan would allow us to secure a victory. So we got to work on my modified plan. If I'm being fully honest, however, we started laying the groundwork for this modification long before the Marshall retirement broke.

Here's what we did to create the avenue for a settlement—the modification of our original plan. Knowing that Governor Edwin Edwards and State Attorney General Richard Ieyoub were up for election—Edwards in a hotly contested race—we used the power of my endorsement as a Louisiana state senator along with the endorsement of other community leaders as leverage to win their support. At the time, my endorsement and that of my political organization was considered one of the strongest in the state. And such an endorsement would give each candidate a stronger standing among black voters.

We secured a commitment from both men that if they won, they would sit down with our team and settle the case to create a black majority Supreme Court district. They also committed to working on settling the companion case, *Clark v. Edwards.* The Clark case focused on obtaining trial and appellate court seats. We did this because I was thinking ahead and trying to identify options. I needed to know we could get a settlement at the state level. The retirement of Justice Marshall simply made that settlement commitment all the more critical.

Another occurrence outside our control, however, aided us. David Duke, the grand wizard of the Ku Klux Klan, made the runoff for governor against Edwards. His presence in the race inspired a record black voter turnout, a turnout that powered both Edwards, Ieyoub, and a record number of black legislators to victory.

Duke's presence, though unpleasant because of the hate he preached and all that he stood for, ironically (at least for him) stimulated a voter turnout that elected a record number of black legislators in the state's history—more than thirty.

Duke's presence was such an anathema to black voters that they began lining up at 4:30 a.m. on election day, a full one and a half hours before the 6:00 a.m. opening of the polls. To say black voters were motivated in that election would be a gross understatement, and it would not do justice to the fire that Duke's presence on the ballot lit in them to stand against racism and hate.

The commitment to settle the case was complicated by the sitting members of the Louisiana Supreme Court, who knew that creating a black majority district would lead to one of them losing their seat. Additionally, members of the state's supreme court and a formidable number of their friends in the state legislature would have to approve any settlement.

This complicated our path. For even with Edwards's and Ieyoub's support, the other folk, those who sought to maintain the status quo, may have had the political clout to block us. So this meant we had to secure support in high places to help us win a settlement. Thus, in my mind, we needed to put our energy into securing the settlement, because the national lay of the land meant putting everything on the line and losing everything. But some members of our legal team thought our past Supreme Court victory meant a certain victory if we returned.

But eventually it came down to the itch of Louisiana Supreme Court members. The case was actually settled during a late-night meeting involving four black state senators, including me, and six of the seven members of the Louisiana Supreme Court. They just wanted to make sure that our goals of obtaining a black seat would not mean any one of them losing their jobs.

One of the black state senators was Gregory Tarver, an undertaker from Shreveport. The most dramatic moment in the meeting was when Tarver, who had a penchant for being brash and blunt, pounded his fist on the table and said, "Listen, as an undertaker, I could care less what any judge thought because the only time I see judges is when I'm embalming them. So I will not settle for anything less than two majority black supreme court districts."

Tarver had effectively upped the ante in dramatic and unexpected fashion. And in equally dramatic fashion, he got up and stormed out of the meeting. At this point, Chief Justice Calogero put an idea on the table: to settle the case, the court would be willing to create a temporary eighth seat on the court that would last for approximately seven years, roughly until the justice whose seat would be affected by the new black seat retired. Additionally, Calogero proposed that, to maintain an odd number of justices for voting purposes, only seven justices would sit for cases at any given time. They would rotate.

This is the settlement our team argued about. Some team members did not want to agree with such a remedy. This was the modified plan. Others felt if we didn't agree to the plan, we'd be back in court and potentially lose everything. My position: settle it, get an African American judge on the court, and move on.

I wasn't willing to take that chance and lose everything we had worked for seven years, and neither was one of my colleagues, the brilliant lawyer and state senator Charles Jones. He suggested we go to DC and speak to the US Justice Department. They had already intervened on our side previously, and Jones believed if we could convince the Justice Department to back our settlement move, we'd have more leverage with members of our own legal team. So he and I flew to DC three to four times to convince the US assistant attorney general John Dunne, to back our settlement move. Jones was a strong supporter of the companion case, *Clark*, which sought to redistrict Louisiana's trial and appellate courts to districts to allow African American representation.

We argued to the Justice Department that a settlement would be less disruptive to the Louisiana judiciary, saving the time and money of three to five more years of litigation. The argument to our own legal team was, hey, we could lose with Clarence Thomas now on the high court. And with the presidential race at the time looking like George H. W. Bush was going to get reelected, that meant potentially another Supreme Court justice would be appointed whose vote would sink our case.

None of this was in the newspapers. No one paid attention to this until we agreed to the settlement and put it before the legislature. But the whole journey shows the power of being aware of everyone's itch—what's most important to them. We provided different arguments for the same case to different audiences because the Justice Department was more concerned with avoiding disruption to state-level judiciaries. Meanwhile, our legal team members were more concerned with getting that additional seat. And once the members of the state's supreme court saw we could get our prize without them having to sacrifice anything, it was a done deal.

Eventually, my modified plan for settling the case won out. The settlement of *Chisom v. Edwards* and its companion case, *Clark v. Edwards*, set the state on a path to more black judges per capita than any other state in the nation. Those victories were responsible for the creation of numerous other majority-black districts throughout the state. As a result, black voters now possessed just as much electoral power as any other citizen to elect their candidates of choice to Louisiana's trial, appellate, and supreme courts.

The combined impact of those two cases brought true and unfettered diversity to Louisiana's judiciary—not to mention the first black supreme court justice, Revius Ortique, who was followed by a black woman serving as chief justice, the Honorable Bernette Joshua Johnson.

The settlement, though not ideal, was the way to go. My legal team colleagues were no fools. They realized modifying our original plan was the way to success. However, there were others who chided our decision. I'm certain at some point over these past decades, they, too, realized the efficacy of the decision to modify our initial legal strategy. But at the time, they were not convinced.

When reflecting on this chapter in my life, I'm reminded that not everybody is going to be down with your plan, project, initiative, proposal, or legislation. And those who are with you may not stick around when you see adjustments need to be made. But when leading, especially when seeking to build intricate coalitions and solve challenges with major business and life ramifications, if you're the captain, and you see victory demands altering your plan, modify, modify, modify, regardless of what others say.

Needless to say, I try my best to remember to always be fluid and flexible enough to make those slight changes and modifications to my plans, recognizing that they could mean the difference between incredible success and abject failure.

GUMBO COALITION RECAP: MODIFICATION

When something happens and you need to modify your plan, whether it's an internal or external factor that's calling you to modify, here's what I suggest you do:

Evaluate if the change is going to benefit or harm your overall objective.

Examine the feasibility and the degree of the modification to your plan. Carefully evaluate the pros and cons. In this instance, the pros should outweigh the cons if you're going to modify your plan. Modification requires calculated and strategic risk-taking.

Communicate the modification and its rationale to stakeholders as necessary and only when needed.

CHAPTER 3

WITH ONE CANOE, WE CAN AVOID THE WATERFALL

A LEADER UNDERSTANDS THE VALUE OF BUILDING CONSENSUS

On May 15, 2003, when I took hold of the reins of the National Urban League, I knew that to get members on board with my vision for the organization I had to build consensus. Some leaders think consensus building involves only bringing outside entities in rhythm with your organization. Not so. Effective leaders know that consensus building, getting everybody on the same page, is just as important, if not more so, within your organization.

Think about it. During World War II, it was certainly critical that the United States had allies in Europe. But if American citizens had not rallied around the cause in mass, there easily could have been a different outcome. And it was this notion of getting everyone moving in the same direction that drove my early moves at the NUL.

One of those consensus-building moves involved overcommunicating the five-point empowerment agenda I had introduced. These five areas of focus—education and youth empowerment, economic empowerment, health and quality of life empowerment, civic engagement and leadership empowerment, and civil rights and racial justice empowerment—became our national foundation, replacing the hodgepodge agendas of NUL affiliates.

We were one organization in name only. One NUL affiliate promoted one set of programs, while another affiliate stressed something totally different. We were all over the place, like a bad baseball pitcher. Balls in the dirt. A few hit batters. A sprinkle of wild pitches. Next thing you know, your opponent is scoring the winning run on a base on balls—a walk, a free pass.

The empowerment agenda became the framework from which the league has executed its programs and continues to operate as such. We've had countless successes in each area, thanks to—drumroll, please—consensus building.

Setting these markers was part of the whole consensus-building process. People have to know what's expected. Not knowing invites chaos. Not expressing and communicating and overcommunicating these expectations literally welcome chaos.

As a new leader taking over an established and iconic institution, I viewed nearly everything as a "new member" orientation session. We had some serious work to do, starting with rebranding the entire organization, making sure to bring all affiliates with their rebel logos and individualized taglines into conformity and consistency. If we were to exhibit excellence, we had to follow the motto repeated over and over again in the movie *Drumline*: One Band, One Sound.

And that's really what consensus building is: getting everyone in your universe (those inside your organization or those entities collaborating with your organization) to move like a well-oiled machine, to make music like One Band, One Sound.

Sports is always the easiest analogy for me because I love all aspects of it. But if you reflect upon the greatest teams of all time, regardless of sport, regardless of whether you were a fan, they all held one thing in common. When they were on that court, diamond, or field, they performed as one. They built consensus, and their actions flowed so seamlessly they often appeared to be performing magic while their opponents seemed to trip over their own feet.

I was not a Boston Celtics fan with the exception of my affection for the legendary Bill Russell. When Larry Bird, Kevin McHale, and the Chief, Robert Parrish, were together competing against the original Showtime Lakers, I was all in for Magic, Kareem, and crew. But as much as I disliked the Celtics, I respected them because they, just like those Showtime Lakers, were the epitome of One Band, One Sound. Their players with vastly different skills meshed beautifully, making them both dangerous and great.

That's what I wanted for the National Urban League—to create a culture where each person with his or her unique skills, talents, passions, and perspectives could buy into a single vision and each contribute to that vision in their own special way.

Everything I did was driven by my desire to create that level of consensus, of buy-in. Even when I eliminated hundreds of different NUL logos in favor of one universal, I did it for this reason. And sure, you may say a little thing like logo consistency couldn't possibly build more of a sense of organizational oneness. I would counter that the Nike Swoosh, McDonald's Golden Arches, and Apple's apple would beg to differ.

But building consensus meant so much more than acceptance of a universal logo. It meant a commitment to those things that historically made the National Urban League stand out. That's why, for me, it was a no-brainer to resurrect the NUL's annual *State of Black America* report.

Far and away one of the most impactful resources produced by any nonprofit organization, the *State of Black America* report provided a vehicle for our organization to speak to those who were not officially members, as well as to local and state elected officials, educators, business leaders, and so many others. It also provided a powerful platform for building consensus because it acted as an organizational playbook from which all members and affiliates could take their marching orders.

Bridging the internal divide—a national office versus local affiliates—was high on my list of items to address. This meant I needed to be on the road regularly, meeting with various entities, stakeholders, collaborators (potential and current), elected officials, and others. Those visits to the local NUL affiliates and the roundtable sessions we had with affiliate leadership went a long way toward replacing the national-office-versus-affiliates paradigm with a feeling that we're all in this thing together.

Incredibly, the internal work we were doing to build consensus emboldened and empowered us to successfully deal with an external challenge that affected us, a challenge, by the way, that affected not solely the league.

In and around 2003, many in the nation questioned the relevance of civil rights organizations. Those who raised this issue argued that all or most playing fields (educational, economic, political, and so on) had been leveled. Thus there was no need for organizations like the National Urban League, NAACP, and others. They had worked themselves out of relevance, some opined. That such a position was blindly inaccurate mattered not. Our organizations still had to plead our case as a regular part of our public discourse.

The relationships among civil rights organizations and leaders was another dangling issue. During this early season of my NUL leadership, Jesse Jackson was at the height of his social and political influence. Kweisi Mfume and, soon after, Benjamin Jealous, headed the NAACP. The Rev. Al Sharpton, who would later form the National Action Network, was rising in prominence as a national civil rights spokesperson.

There was a sense that these groups and individuals regularly competed for the limelight. This divisiveness often led to donating entities playing one organization or leader against another. The thinking was, if you donated to the NAACP, there was no need to donate to the National Urban League or to an Asian or Latino advocacy group.

When confronted with that question, my response was, "Keep giving to the NAACP, to this Asian group, or that Latino group because what they do may be complementary to the efforts that fall under our five-point empowerment agenda. But know that all these organizations do different things. Let me tell you what we do at the National Urban League . . ."

I dearly wanted to work toward changing that us-versus-them mentality, the competitive paradigm that undermined our ability to build a culture of collaborative empowerment.

To execute this consensus-building plan, I had several one-on-one conversations, personal meetings, and phone calls. I engaged in open and honest dialogue about past realities, present challenges, and future possibilities. I invested personal time, energy, and sweat equity into executing this vision of a new collaborative, strategic mind-set for civil rights—our new way of operating. It was a consensus based on unity, not unanimity.

From this work, we successfully created a compact among me, Rev. Sharpton, Ben Jealous of the NAACP, and Melanie Campbell, executive director and chief executive officer of the National Coalition on Black Civic Participation Inc., to work together with the Obama administration.

As President Obama's second term began, our group would regularly meet with the president, as well as with many others who were included along the way.

One could ask what the benefits were to the community of our approach.

I would say emphatically that the stimulus plan produced by the Obama administration, which helped bring the economy back, included provisions for job training, housing assistance, and the like. All of these impacted in an incredibly positive way African Americans and all Americans.

I would add that the Affordable Care Act, otherwise known as Obamacare, included within it an expansion of Medicaid that brought health-care benefits to millions of African Americans and others who were previously without coverage.

Additionally, President Obama appointed a record number of African American federal judges. In his second term, at our prodding, he took significant steps to push an agenda of criminal justice reform, with Attorney General Eric Holder leading the way.

I am absolutely clear that our advocacy in those ongoing meetings with President Obama, Valerie Jarrett, Roderick Johnson, Eric Holder, and Sally Yates, among others, made a difference in how the Obama administration approached these important issues.

Additionally, the Recovery Act was about a year old when Jealous and I went to the White House and prodded and pleaded with President Obama to introduce a jobs bill that was more targeted in its approach. In other words, we pushed him to make the plan more targeted to help black and brown communities. President Obama said he would do so, and as a man of his word, he did just that—only to see it blocked by the Republican-dominated House of Representatives.

We pushed the president very hard at the beginning of his second term because the first appointees did not reflect the diversity we needed. Again, he responded in a big way. I was in every one of those meetings for eight years; Rev. Al Sharpton and I saw firsthand how such advocacy created the openings for change. At the beginning of Obama's second term, our advocacy led to a more diverse cabinet, with Anthony Foxx being named Transportation secretary, Jeh Johnson being appointed Homeland Security secretary, Julian Castro being appointed HUD secretary, and Mel Watt being named to head the Federal Housing Finance Agency.

We vowed that we would not participate in public bickering with each other or with President Obama. We committed to publicly showing a united front. This accord is not only ongoing to this day, but the commitment to a more collaborative and supportive public face has also led to a more collaborative and supportive behind-the-scenes relationship. I am certainly proud of the contributions I made to executing the founding of a new working reality.

REBUILD NEW ORLEANS NOW

Building consensus is not an optional part of effective leadership. It's central to your ability to get all necessary forces aligned and moving in concert. Of the numerous examples that come to mind, the one that resonates most with me is my work as New Orleans' mayor gathering support for a huge capital bond program in 1995.

The challenge: no one was rowing in the same direction.

In New Orleans politics, it had become tradition that various groups would fight to place their capital bond issues on the ballot. Each group would then go into *Survivor* mode, competing with all other bonds, hoping to stifle support for "rivals" while recruiting supporters for its own cause. What would ultimately happen each election season was that some of the bonds passed while others didn't, meaning some groups got what they wanted while others got nothing.

The problem as I saw it was each group approached this bond battle as a zero-sum game. That is, if the other group wins, my group loses. This is an approach antithetical to consensus and coalition building. It's dog-eat-dog, each person or group for themselves. And just prior to the 1995 local elections, like clockwork, the groups and industries that needed taxpayer money for their initiatives entered the ring ready to knock out any and all others seeking funding for their own projects.

It reminded me of a saying I learned from a veteran senator I served with: "One canoe can avoid the waterfall." Translation: If everyone is doing their own thing, and there is no cohesion or commitment to a particular vision or path, then it's every person for themselves. As a result, the chances of a negative outcome are increased tremendously. But when folk come together on common ground, or in the same canoe, they can then avoid danger and steer toward their common goal.

In the case of the various city entities looking for capital dollars, each constituent group had their own canoe, and everyone was in danger of the waterfall.

The education contingent wanted to expand schools and facilities with millions of dollars earmarked for physical upgrades. The neighborhood lobby wanted funds for much-needed street repairs. Those representing the city's recreation interests hoped to access capital dollars to improve or build playgrounds and swimming pools.

Then there was the shipping industry, arguing that the amount of commerce they generated warranted their call for the city to pay for port infrastructure improvements. But the hospitality industry, which is huge in New Orleans, argued from that same position for an expansion of the convention center.

They were all committed to doing business the old way, the traditional way, with each group fighting for their lone bond, knowing full well that, when placed next to all the other contenders, more than half would take the loser plunge over the waterfall.

I was determined to change this losing paradigm, where groups cooked in their separate pots. I mean, imagine for a minute everybody's trying to make gumbo but one chef cooks only the roux and refuses to partner with those cooking the chicken and seafood. Or the one with the okra throws his or her ingredient into the pot all by itself, no roux, no celery, no crab, no sausage in sight, yet expecting gumbo at the end of the process. It makes no sense, but this is exactly what New Orleans politics looked like. My job as the city's leader was to bring these groups together in consensus, so that all could achieve a win-win result—gumbo.

I shared this goal with several of the key players involved, leaders of various industries each seeking capital dollars, each proposing his or her own bond initiative. My logic was simple: going it alone is a crapshoot that rarely works out well for the smaller, less powerful entities. And even the big dogs were never guaranteed to see their bonds pass on any given year. My proposal: place all initiatives together in consensus. I also had to challenge them to think big.

I wish I would have recorded some of their initial reactions. Some laughed uncontrollably. They said how crazy and impossible an idea that was. One or two bristled with anger at the idea of having to partner with groups they saw as rivals. But what was really at work was fear. They feared the unknown. No one had dared try to pull off passing a capital bond so big. They surmised that if each separate bond was thrown into the pot together, it would produce the largest bond in the history of the city—$350 million to be exact. And they were right.

Those who pointed this out argued the number itself would spell doom for all involved. Voters wouldn't go for it.

One interesting subtext to this story occurred within the New Orleans business community. On one hand, there was Ian Arnoff, president of First National Bank of Commerce and a prominent supporter of my opponent when I ran for mayor. Arnoff was a dignified statesmanlike figure who cut a regal, debonair figure of grace and reasonableness.

On the other side was Jim Bob Moffet, the swashbuckling CEO of Freeport-McMoRan. Moffet could be blunt and raw. Arnoff, who was always a stickler for the King's English, was always a buttoned-up banker.

Arnoff took the position that the needs of the schools far outweighed other issues and said the members of New Orleans' business community would not go for my bond consolidation plan. With this declaration, Arnoff set himself up as a bit of an adversary.

Moffet, on the other hand, invited me to his office and gave me advice on how to best sell the package to members of the Business Council of New Orleans. Moffet also privately railed against those who disagreed with my approach, calling them small thinkers, and gave me very public credit for thinking big, saying it was the only way the city would win.

Moreover, Moffet helped me form my presentation. I knew if the business community opposed the combined bond issue it would be difficult to pass. But I calculated we could still win a majority because needs of neighborhoods and schools and users of neighborhood pools were all constituents. While downtown interests viewed these as separate entities, the community residents looked at the combined bonds as a way to improve the quality of life.

But even before that, they said there was no way I could get all groups on board to agree to come together, especially since a bond that big would require a hike in taxes. Voters certainly wouldn't go for that.

Well that I knew, each group's itch came into play big-time. I let them know that alone your group doesn't have the resources to guarantee the votes to access the funds you need. But if you partner together, then the marketing efforts of one group will become the marketing efforts of all groups. I also told them that the groups you see as rivals are really partners; for your effort to fully work, you need those other groups funded and operating at maximum capacity. You need to build consensus with your so-called rivals.

I had to sweet-talk, cajole, employ theatrics, and convince all of their interests to come together. I played political hardball. As a popular new mayor with the strongest political operation, I told them that if they did not come along, we would go to the voters without their projects included.

In the end, they saw the light and understood the wisdom of going about this search for capital funds together rather than as lone wolves.

Our capital bond initiative called Rebuild New Orleans Now! received near unanimous support from the business council, the daily newspaper, organized labor, faith-based organizations, and the very important United Teachers of New Orleans, the city's largest public employee union.

In the end, the unified bond turned out to be a big victory for the city. Not only did the initiative win the day at the ballot box, but the results far surpassed expectations. To the point about the bond being so big it would scare off voters, I countered that because the bond was so big there wasn't a single sector that didn't have a stake. And because everyone was invested in its success, everyone, working in collaboration and consensus, would promote it in their spheres of influence. It was a marvel of consensus building.

And, surprisingly to many, the largest bond issue in the history of the city, Rebuild New Orleans Now!, passed with nearly 70 percent of the vote. We made gumbo, and everybody ate well!

And, yes, the bond did require a tax hike. But I sold it to voters by letting them know about all of the extra jobs they would enjoy from a passed bond. I promised the most aggressive effort in the city's history, and told them that it would only cost them a mere extra dime a day: an extremely inexpensive investment in a host of community-empowering initiatives. Did I mention the bond passed with nearly 70 percent of the vote?

I should add that for me to even attempt such a feat was a big baller move. I mention this not so much as a personal brag but as proof of how critical it is to get off to a fast start with a solid plan. Because of my public safety plan's success in my first year, I built up enough momentum, goodwill, public trust, and confidence to attempt what some said was impossible.

I have to make this point again, because it's just that important. Working in my favor was the fact that I knew the city and the people, and I knew what each of the primary constituent groups wanted and needed. I knew everybody's itch.

(Quick leadership aside—an effective leader puts in the time to learn and intimately know the landscape in which he or she has to work. This means getting to know the people and organizations, along with their priorities, resources, and challenges.)

With that knowledge, and with the people skills I had been building upon since my days crossing the ditch, I went to work. I tried to convince these many constituent groups to abandon their multiple doomed canoes and join together, to increase the chances of every group's success. We had to make changes to the bond bill to make this happen, but that was simply part of the challenge—we made changes, concessions, and additions to make sure everyone in this potential coalition viewed the program as a benefit to themselves.

This is not to suggest that everybody was ready to jump on board this consensus train without a fight. There were some who were dead set against joining forces with others. With them, I took a different tack. I forced everyone to the table in part because I had the political machinery to pass whatever I wanted and almost certainly doom whatever I opposed. I let the fence-riders and skeptics know that if they didn't jump on board our coalition bond train, they were going to be left behind to fend for themselves. And the prospects of their success were going to be slim and none. In short, they got on board.

In the end, the plan eventually adopted included something for everyone. It was truly a gumbo. And no one group could get what they wanted or needed without supporting the entire pot of gumbo—the entire capital bond program.

I had to use every skill in my pocket and every trick in the book to get these disparate groups to come to the table as unified collaborators in that one canoe. Some I had to force to think differently, challenging them verbally. Others required, for lack of a better term, sweet talk. The bottom line was I had to communicate with each group in a way that made the most sense for the preferred outcome. And in the end, everybody felt that they had won.

And that's what's at the heart of consensus building: making sure everyone sees their participation as a win.

Reflecting on that victory always calls to mind a quote: "Leaders have three fundamental responsibilities: they craft a vision, they build alignment, and they champion execution." I find it quite apropos that this quote has no name other than "anonymous" attached to it.

Recently, the city of New Orleans attempted this same consensus-building approach to pass a bond. The city's zoo director, Ron

Forman, had tried to get a bond passed two years prior. It failed. Afterwards, he told me, "Next go-round, we're going to take a page out of your book." That next election season, Forman and others created a consensus rather than having individual entities go it alone in their quest for capital dollars. Their results may have been surprising to some, but not to me. Their combined efforts passed. They realized that by rowing individually, separate canoes risked disaster. But together, in one canoe, they each could avoid the waterfall.

GUMBO COALITION RECAP: CONSENSUS BUILDING

Consensus building requires knowing where everybody's itch is.

Here is a method I use to build consensus.

I identify a common objective or a common threat.

I communicate one-on-one to allow people to be heard and to give me the opportunity to persuade.

I adopt a win-win approach but recognize that win-win means I don't win everything.

If consensus building doesn't work, then I use disruption and dynamite. a) As a leader, I make my best efforts to achieve consensus by reason, persuasion, and sweet talk. If that proves ineffective, I reserve the right to do what I can to achieve the objective. This means I might have to proceed without you and forget about a win-win. b) The risk of using dynamite is my opponent may have their own stick of dynamite.

SECTION TWO

"SENATOR, I CALL THEM PEOPLE"

My parents' successful professional careers gave our family financial stability. There was always food and shelter, but no frills and no pocket money. Moreover, my mother was a working mom for as many years as I can remember. While my father was serving as a lawyer, legislator, judge, and then as mayor, my mother was cultivating a twenty-eight-year career at Xavier University. Prior to that she was a second-grade teacher at Dunn Elementary School, which was located in the Desire Public Housing Development. Amazingly, she was able to be an incredible nurturer of her five children while also serving as a permanent fixture in New Orleans' civic life.

But my mother and father were as far from pretentious as human beings could be. To label them as down-to-earth people would be an understatement. Ernest Nathan "Dutch" Morial and his bride, Sybil Haydel Morial, centered their priorities on faith, family, education, and service. I'm not sure the notions of being ostentatious and putting on airs ever entered their minds. Their lives and their children's lives were consumed with striving for excellence in daily tasks (work and school) and serving the community in some capacity. Sundays were all about church, followed by our family's weekly visits to our grandparents' homes.

Our tight-knit family included my three sisters, Julie, Cheri, and Monique, and my brother, Jacques. We lived in our home with two girls in one bedroom, two boys in another bedroom, and my baby sister, Monique, in our parents' bedroom until she was three years old and we moved to a larger house.

While residing in Pontchartrain Park, we lived tight, to say the least. Pontchartrain Park was a historic subdivision built in the 1950s created by city fathers specifically for black residents and to keep blacks from seeking to integrate into white neighborhoods, namely the neighboring Gentilly Woods. A ditch separated the two.

In our Pontchartrain Park home, there were three window AC units: one in our parents' bedroom, one in the living room, and the other in the den. They were all hand-me-downs from my grandparents. There was also a converted screen porch that became our small den. On our new color television, we watched men land on the moon, the first Super Bowl, weekly editions of *Soul Train*, and Muhammad Ali's fight against Zora Folley, his last fight before his life and title were stripped away.

I'm painting this picture to explain that our upbringing in those days was modest and not extravagant in the least, even as my parents were prominent civic and community leaders. The upshot of such a modest upbringing was that we learned how to live in and survive the formidable New Orleans heat and humidity.

This very simple, faith-family-service existence instilled in my siblings and me the notion of humble service, hard work, commitment borne of divine responsibilities, and honoring and respecting the humanity of all. Regardless.

It's amazing how those attributes prepared me for so many of my life experiences, such as my time serving as a Louisiana state senator. The district whose seat I won was statistically the most diverse in the state. The district had been created by incumbents who carved up and cut out whole swaths of their own districts that did not suit their political tastes. It was simultaneously home to the most liberal and most conservative individuals and families in Louisiana. That district had folks from every walk of life, every religious persuasion, every socioeconomic stratum, and every race.

EQUALITY MARCHES ON

One of the most notable characteristics of my senate district was that it included a large array of individuals representing every gender and sexual identity in existence. I was cognizant of and a champion for LGBTQ rights long before it became popular or politically expedient. Even before I was elected to the senate, I was one of two African American civic and political leaders to ride as grand marshal in what was then called the Gay Pride Parade.

For me, support of LGBTQ rights was basic and fundamental. Why? Because I rejected the hollow interpretation of Christianity that used scripture to support bigoted opinions of LGBTQ individuals. I chose instead to embrace the ultimate commandment of my faith: to love one's neighbors as I love myself.

I recognized that throughout history individuals have used scripture to justify all manner of systems that in no way reflected foundational spiritual principles of loving and respecting one's fellow human beings. Neither at that time nor since have I allowed myself to let someone, no matter how revered, to use words as ammunition to justify and support their prejudices. I'm not here for that.

Today's general level of acceptance of LGBTQ members is light-years from where the country was in the early '90s.[1] In the 1990s there existed only two known gay-straight alliance clubs in US high schools. Today, you would be hard pressed to find a high school in a major urban area without such an organization. On January 29, 1990, *Time* magazine coined the term *outing* while reporting on Michelangelo Signorile's campaign to publicly identify LGBTQ celebrities and elected officials who were then still living lives "in the closet." Though Signorile, an outspoken gay rights activist, reportedly did not try to shame those he named, any person today actively "outing" public figures would either be met with disdain or a big yawn. It shows just how far we've come.

It was a vastly different world, with policies restricting the immigration of lesbians and gays into the United States on the books up until 1990.[2] So when I introduced hate crime legislation based on sexual orientation in 1992 in the Deep South, it was considered a daring and risky professional move. To me, however, it was simply an elected official standing up for his constituents—wanting all district residents to have the space and opportunity to live safe and full lives and wanting those who would impinge upon that safety with hate-filled violence to be held accountable by the law.

After I introduced the legislation on the floor of the Louisiana Senate, I was joined at the podium by a colleague. It was senate custom for any senator who had questions for the senator at the podium to come forward and stand side by side to ask the questions, sharing the one microphone. There was no throwing verbal shots or snide comments from a safe distance. A senator would have to make the walk to the podium, and most times look the person in the eye, when asking their question.

But on that day in 1992, there was my fellow freshman senator Max Jordan, standing beside me at the podium, ready to ask his questions.

My recollection of our conversation went like this:

"Senator Morial, I don't understand your bill," Jordan said.

"What do you not understand, Senator?"

After a moment of hemming and hawing, Jordan got to the point: "Senator, is this a queer bill?"

Immediately, the whole senate chamber fell silent, a silence broken by Jordan as he repeated his question: "Senator, is this a queer bill?"

"I'm not sure I understand your question," I responded, more out of surprise that Jordan actually asked such a question out loud than any lack of understanding of what my colleague was attempting to say.

His response to me? "Well, Senator, what would you call 'em?"

"Senator, I call them people."

Immediately, Jordan's face went red and he returned to his seat.

The bill would pass the senate overwhelmingly and die in the house. The following year, 1993, I introduced an LGBTQ equality bill barring discrimination in housing and employment based on sexual orientation. It passed in the senate and died in the house. It's remarkable that, twenty-five years later, the US House has finally passed federal regulation that mirrors the bill I introduced a quarter of a century earlier. As of this writing, it awaits action in the US Senate.

IS ALL BLOOD EQUAL?

The incident took *me* back to my childhood when, at age ten, I witnessed my father endure a similar experience during his time as a Louisiana legislator.

In the early 1940s, when the United States entered World War II, donating blood was becoming a way for people to express their patriotic commitment to their country. Even though it was a black man in the 1930s, named Dr. Charles Drew, who made blood donations possible, blacks nationwide were banned from giving blood. If it weren't for the procedure he invented to process and preserve blood plasma, blood transfusions would have not been possible. Using his own inventions and expertise as his guide, Dr. Drew developed large-scale blood banks early in World War II. In fact, even before the United States entered the fray, Americans sent blood overseas to support Allied forces via a program led by Drew, the "Plasma for Britain" project.

Dr. Drew's innovations led to the founding of the American Red Cross Blood Bank. He even managed two of the nation's largest blood banks. And even though blacks were eventually allowed to donate blood, their gift was still a segregated commodity: black blood could be used only for blacks and white blood for whites. Dr. Drew eventually resigned his post with the American Red Cross in protest of their dogged commitment to continue the practice.

But in 1950 the Red Cross finally bowed to the supremacy of science—and common sense—which proved no biological difference between the segregated bloods. Yet in Louisiana some nineteen additional years later, blood was still being classified by race and segregated in its storage and use.

To my father, a state representative at the time, this practice made no sense. He introduced legislation in the late 1960s to bring this blood apartheid to an end. More specifically, his legislation sought to end the labeling of black and white blood.

I happened to be at the state capital at age ten, hanging out with my father the week his bill was up for discussion. On the day my father manned the podium to introduce his "delabeling" legislation, I was in the legislative chamber, sitting at my father's desk. Immediately after stating his case, my father encountered the remarks of his colleague, Rep. Archie Davis, whose words that day would make national headlines.

"I would see my family die and go to eternity before I would see them have one drop of nigger blood in them," Davis declared.[3]

What my father brought to the table after that moment and during the entirety of his professional and political career was a powerful combination of strength and compassion. It's this same combination that I have relied upon in each of my leadership roles. Leading with one and not the other is not only inadvisable, it's dangerous. A leader who operates out of strength but lacks compassion becomes a dictator, an authoritarian. Compassionate leaders who lack the strength to get things done, the strength to make the difficult decisions, stay stuck in their feelings, never moving forward.

You need both qualities to make decisions under pressure, and a leader must master them daily. You need both qualities to successfully deal with surprise, that constant life companion for anyone attempting to do anything of meaning or significance. Both qualities when combined become an indispensable tool for the transformational leader. The three chapters in this section highlight this dynamic duo (strength and compassion) as a leadership principle, along with the skills needed for making decisions under pressure and dealing with surprise.

SECTION TWO OF *THE GUMBO COALITION* HIGHLIGHTS THREE KEY LEADERSHIP LESSONS:

- "They're Not Refugees, Dammit"—A Leader Shows Strength through Compassion
- "Know When to Hold 'Em, Know When to Fold 'Em"—A Leader Is Skilled at Decision-Making under Pressure
- "Get Ready for the Big Payback"—A Leader Is Not Paralyzed by the Unexpected

The following chapters and the qualities they illuminate focus on showing strength through compassion, which is a level of mental and emotional "toughness" many leaders fail to recognize. This section also focuses on making decisions under pressure, because pressure is something a leader deals with daily. Moreover, this section shows the payoff of being able to combine strength and compassion with the ability to perform under pressure—a combination that will shield you from being paralyzed by fear when the unexpected comes knocking at your door.

CHAPTER 4

THEY'RE NOT REFUGEES, DAMMIT

A LEADER SHOWS STRENGTH THROUGH COMPASSION

On Monday, August 29, 2005, the day Hurricane Katrina hit, I was in New Orleans, having traveled from New York City where we had moved. I was there to offer remarks at the funeral of Clarence L. Barney Jr., former president of the Urban League of Greater New Orleans. When the funeral, which was held at the Dillard University Chapel, was about two-thirds complete, my communications director signaled me and said, "We have to leave now. The hurricane headed this way has gone from a category one to a category five."

Here it's important for me to share a word on just who Clarence L. Barney Jr. was.

Barney was one of New Orleans' most prominent civil rights leaders ever.[1] He led the Urban League of New Orleans from 1967 to 1996. Barney was an energetic and talkative man who spent many hours with me before I interviewed for the final time for the presidency of the National Urban League.

One of those many preparation sessions, which I will always remember, took place in his kitchen as a violent rainstorm raged outdoors and his wife served us a delicious gumbo.

Barney gave me insight that was indispensable on my last interview.

I owe Clarence L. Barney Jr. greatly for my eventual garnering of the presidency of the National Urban League. The time and attention he graciously and generously shared with me he also gave to countless others in the city whom he deemed were serious about local and national leadership.

It was no surprise to me or anyone else attending that his funeral was a grand celebration, as civic and political leaders of all stripes gathered in that chapel. As one would expect at funerals for dignitaries who spent their lives nurturing and grooming and supporting others in their quests to be better community servants, the list of dignitaries speaking that day was quite lengthy.

So it remains stunning to me whenever I reflect on that moment that a celebration of his life, a celebration so grand and uplifting, could be succeeded by the tragedy of Hurricane Katrina just forty-eight hours later. Barney was an important figure and one of the few individuals I had taken into full confidence when I decided to pursue the job of National Urban League president. He was also the first black to serve as chairman of the LSU Board of Supervisors, and he has a building named after him on the Louisiana State University campus. I can't say enough about him. And at his homegoing, I was not able to say nearly as much as I would have liked because of the news I had been given about the coming storm.

For a brief second I was in disbelief, because when we arrived in the city that morning it was a gorgeous day with no sign of bad weather. "Okay," I responded, "let's go, but first I want to run by and check on my mother."

When we got to her house, I turned on the TV to check the news. It was then I fully realized what was coming. I told my mother she had to leave with me and head to Baton Rouge to stay with my sister. Being the strong, stubborn woman that she is, her initial answer was no as she headed up the stairs, then adding in true New Orleans fashion, "That storm isn't coming this way."

I told my communications director I wasn't leaving the house until my mother left. After some more thought, my mother finally agreed to leave. My mother followed me as I headed to the airport. She then veered toward much higher, safer ground in Baton Rouge to stay with my sister.

When the storm hit, my mother's house was completely flooded, as were the homes of my two sisters who lived in the city, as well as the home I owned in New Orleans. All things considered, we were fortunate. So many others were not. Death and destruction engulfed the entire region.

At home in New York, I watched the Hurricane Katrina coverage on the news with my wife, Michelle. She and I have been married since 1999, after meeting five years earlier at one of my earliest press conferences as mayor. She was a brand new reporter. She was attractive and spunky and caught my eye immediately.

As we watched the news and happenings in New Orleans, what I saw not only broke my heart, it made my blood boil. I don't know if I have ever been that angry in my life, before or since Katrina, as I was when I saw people stranded at the city's convention center. I was pissed to no end hearing that those tens of thousands of people who poured into the Superdome and the convention center were without food, water, and medical supplies.[2] I knew for a fact that in 1998, when I was mayor coordinating a hurricane response, we had those locations stocked with plenty of supplies for the displaced.

My anger didn't stop there. In those critical hours and days following Katrina making landfall, I saw a heart-wrenching spectacle of callousness, ineptitude, and a gross lack of leadership. The three people in the entire nation with the most power and responsibility to act decisively to save lives and restore hope were each actively allowing incompetence to rule the day. The city's mayor, Ray Nagin, along with Louisiana governor Kathleen Blanco and President George W. Bush, played the blame game regarding the lack of an adequate response to help those most victimized. Each pointed fingers at the others, allowing party politics to guide their moves, rather than the strength and compassion the people of New Orleans needed.

Though my mother was able to make it out safely, I personally knew many who lost parents. I saw the Superdome and the convention center that bares my father's name turned into houses of horror. And still nothing but weakness and callousness coming from Nagin, Blanco, and Bush.

In the earliest days of Hurricane Katrina, there was the absolute courage of individual citizens on display, individuals creating makeshift rafts out of doors, refrigerators, and anything that could float to rescue neighbors in need, distress, and danger. Then, there was the US Coast Guard using helicopters to rescue trapped and desperate individuals and families off rooftops of homes ravaged by rising waters. These brave rescues occurred throughout the city's Ninth Ward and other areas in New Orleans.

The National Urban League honored the US Coast Guard at our Equal Opportunity Day Dinner in 2005. For had it not been for their Herculean efforts and the courage of many individual citizens, thousands more may have perished. Those Coast Guard members and individual citizens evidenced strength through compassion at a time of great human need.

And sure, Nagin and Blanco were right to call out the lack of federal help for its own citizens in need. When Lt. Gen. Russell Honoré was assigned commander of the Joint Task Force Katrina responsible for coordinating military relief efforts, the people of New Orleans were living as if they were in the bowels of a slave ship. I stated emphatically to anyone who would listen that the mistreatment and lack of a compassionate response to New Orleans residents in misery would not happen if this were New York City or Miami Beach, Florida. The federal government failed its citizens residing in New Orleans.

Where was the local and statewide leadership as New Orleans existed under martial law with no water, no electricity, and no Internet, leaving the city dark as a forest at night? The strength and compassion New Orleanians needed in their many hours of need were missing in action from the leaders who could have made a difference.

With the city sitting in a natural basin, it was a natural and human-made disaster just waiting to happen. That natural basin meant some of the city existed below sea level, with low-income communities tending to exist at the very lowest levels. When that disaster did happen in the form of Hurricane Katrina, between twelve hundred and nearly two thousand people lost their lives, almost six hundred from chronic disease "exacerbated by the storm" and roughly four hundred from drowning.[3]

We know that an estimated four hundred thousand New Orleans residents were permanently displaced, having to leave their city to make a new life for themselves and their families in cities they were unfamiliar with, places like Houston, Dallas, and Atlanta.[4] We know that the unprecedented destructive nature of the storm produced a damage price tag of hundreds of billions of dollars.

But those who remained in the city, those who survived the storm and the inhumane conditions within the Superdome, had to somehow deal with a city whose insufficient levee system had been severely compromised. A city where entire neighborhoods had been reduced to rubble. A city that had several business leaders conspiring to remake the city by destroying traditional communities of color, thereby further displacing hundreds and even thousands more native New Orleanians.

Had I been mayor during that terrible time, I would have sent city police to all local grocery stores to open them up after calling the store owners and letting them know their entire inventory would be purchased by the city and distributed to the people by city staff and police.

I would have demanded and used every resource to ensure that water, food, and medical supplies were available at the Ernest N.

Morial Convention Center and the Superdome, which had become shelters of last resort. I know this well because in 1998 as mayor I led the response to Hurricane Georges.

Though Georges was no Katrina, both facilities, the Superdome and the convention center, were then used as shelters of last resort. In the days leading up to the arrival of Hurricane Georges, we turned over every stone to ensure those places were stocked with food, water, and medical supplies. Additionally, before television programming was interrupted, I issued a call to all residents of the Greater New Orleans Metropolitan area for additional doctors, nurses, medical assistants, and other medical professionals to come and volunteer at the Superdome and the convention center because we simply didn't have enough on staff.

And volunteers came out by the droves. It was heartwarming to see such an example of the positive aspects of the human spirit.

I was absolutely livid when I was called to a meeting at the White House the Saturday after Katrina. Why the anger? Michael Chertoff, who was then the secretary of homeland security, was present, and when I asked him why they were not airlifting food, water, and supplies to the Superdome, his answer stopped me in my tracks.

A high government official responded by telling me that there was no place to land a helicopter at the Superdome, thus making such transports impossible. I responded, "There's a helipad at the dome. Who is giving you your misinformation?" I'm not certain if I yelled my response or managed to keep a calm, cool exterior. But either way, I was beyond livid, because it showed gross incompetence on local and federal levels. And because of that misinformation, countless people were caused to suffer unnecessarily for longer than they had to. To this day, when remembering that conversation, my blood boils all over again.

What I would not have done was let politics and ego block efforts to help and minister to those in need.

I was still hot a week and a half after the storm hit when I visited Houston to meet with displaced New Orleanians sheltered in the

Astrodome. Both then senator and future president Barack Obama and former president Bill Clinton were there. Together, the three of us provided whatever comfort our presence could provide. But I grew hotter still hearing all the talking heads and politicians refer to these displaced US citizens as refugees.

After visiting Houston several weeks later, I learned that a group of business leaders from New Orleans had met in Dallas and were working with the DC-based Urban Land Institute to develop a recovery plan for the city, which seemed, on its face, to be the right thing to do. I later learned that the plan would recommend that large parts of New Orleans East and the Ninth Ward be turned into lagoons and green space requiring a forced displacement of more than one hundred thousand mostly African American New Orleans residents and the destruction of historically black neighborhoods like Pontchartrain Park, where I grew up.

My phone and email lit up like a Fourth of July fireworks celebration, with community leaders calling to ask me for help to convince leadership to oppose the plan. I was shocked that New Orleans business leaders would support a plan that smacked of ethnic cleansing of a people who had lost everything and were now on their backs.

The forces confronting this plan, however, were not deterred or intimidated by the lack of humanity they faced coming from the individuals who conceived the plan. These opposing forces were loud and resolute.

As soon as this plan for the literal and symbolic ethnic cleansing of New Orleans leaked, but before its formal announcement, I received a call from a midlevel employee from the Urban Land Institute. The individual said she had been instructed to call me as a courtesy to brief me on the plan. I told her if the announced plan was the same as what had been leaked, I would publicly and vigorously oppose the plan.

I then traveled to my hometown as opposition to the plan mounted and held a large rally at St. Maria Goretti Catholic Church in New Orleans East. The church had no electricity or lights, and its carpet had been pulled up. Rally attendees sat on folding chairs rather than regal church pews. St. Maria Goretti Catholic Church was one of the few buildings open, and they made themselves available to their community in need and hurting.

I felt as many did that it was a mistake for there to be plans to bring the city back that was not inclusive or built around collaboration. Not only was that the gumbo spirit in me, it was just plain common sense and human decency.

As a result of our advocacy, the ill-conceived plan was dead on arrival and derisively mocked as the Dallas Plan. St. Maria Goretti Catholic Church and the residents who made up that coalition of opposition forces displayed strength through compassion.

Meanwhile, the National Urban League decided to dedicate its efforts to providing job placement and housing assistance services to the hundreds of thousands of displaced residents. We raised roughly $5 million and immediately distributed it to our affiliates in Houston, Dallas, Memphis, Birmingham, Atlanta, and to several other affiliates who were helping displaced New Orleans residents. We also helped to organize with Black Entertainment Television a telethon, which raised millions for the American Red Cross and featured numerous prominent celebrities. These National Urban League affiliates displayed strength through compassion by providing all manner of service, while our own New Orleans affiliate was flooded out of its building and had to take up temporary residence in Baton Rouge.

The speech I gave at St. Maria Goretti Catholic Church was titled "Turn the Lights On." Also, two months earlier, I had returned to my alma mater, Georgetown University Law School, and delivered a message titled "The Katrina Bill of Rights," which was also presented as testimony before the US Congress.

But it must be said that those official, elected leaders on the local, state, and federal levels showed neither strength nor compassion in the immediate aftermath of Hurricane Katrina. This monumental failure of leadership had devastatingly disastrous results on those lives lost and those forever changed. It impacted Nagin, Blanco, and Bush as well. Eventually, however, Bush and Blanco led efforts to appropriate millions in state and federal dollars to rebuild New Orleans and southern Louisiana. And though there are certainly many factors that go into defining an elected official's legacy, there is little doubt that the inaction of Nagin, Blanco, and Bush regarding Hurricane Katrina left an indelible mark upon their political careers.

Nagin, on the other hand, was convicted of numerous federal crimes and sentenced to ten years in federal prison, the first New Orleans mayor in the city's three-hundred-year history to be indicted and convicted. His ineffectiveness, incompetence, and buffoonery were stunning and embarrassing.

The Hurricane Katrina nonresponse from leaders forever changed the game for hurricane preparation and how government leadership deals with other major challenges. After Katrina, the nation witnessed substantial changes in how elected officials respond to big weather crises and in how FEMA responds. Katrina sent a powerful message to mayors, governors, and presidents that you have to respond with strength and compassion.

I haven't spoken with him, but I'm sure that in the back of his mind when Hurricane Harvey hit, Houston's mayor, Sylvester Turner, was saying, "I'm not having a Katrina in my city."

And he didn't. Turner's response to the horrors and challenges of his city's own major weather emergency was textbook perfect, because he offered strength through compassion both early and often throughout the ordeal. We saw this in the response to Superstorm Sandy in the Northeast too—leaders putting party politics aside for the good of those impacted and hurting from the storm.

Unfortunately, exhibiting strength through compassion has yet to become standard for all leaders. Puerto Rico is a modern-day Katrina with hurting people being ignored due to such a poor response. Amazingly, most Americans don't realize Puerto Ricans are US citizens. That, plus the fact that Puerto Rico is a territory, may explain why there hasn't been as much negative blowback as in Katrina's aftermath. But the fact remains that neither strength nor compassion has been offered to our fellow citizens there.

Strength through compassion is important because the essence of leadership is service. Strength through compassion demonstrates you have an understanding, a feeling, a concern for people. Strength compels decisiveness and moves you to act with purpose, to respond in real time to the needs of people. Compassion compels you to act urgently because you feel the people's pain and put all BS and bureaucratic red tape aside to alleviate that pain as best you can.

In the Katrina case, a good leader would say, "I have the ability to channel all of the anger and pain in the city into responsive action." When Katrina hit, I remember thinking, "Man, I'm glad I'm not in charge having to deal with all the madness." But two to three days into the fiasco, I was chomping at the bit, wishing to God I was in charge. There's absolutely no way I would have let people starve and go without food and water. There's no way I would have put politics and egos before caring for a hurting people.

At the time, I never said out loud that I would have done a much better job at handling the situation than then mayor Nagin. But the fact is I would have.

When giving speeches on leadership, I tell audiences all the time, if you're going to be a leader you have to know the people you profess to lead. Are you sensitive to the fact you're leading people who are earning only $35,000 a year? Do you have a feel for what they're dealing with? Do you factor that into your decision-making? That's where much of your strength and compassion comes from.

As head of the National Urban League, I worry all the time if I'm paying people sufficiently. I refuse to reduce the benefits to our health plan even when it will save the NUL a little money, because I factor in the human cost. As a leader, strength through compassion shows up through your decision-making. Leaders, especially in business, always have to evaluate the fiscal impact of any move. But you should also evaluate the human impact, especially when making major decisions. That's what compassion is when you're a leader.

And it doesn't mean you constantly sacrifice profits. But it does mean the human impact is always considered—you spend as much analysis on the human element as you do the financial.

My family and I were lucky in that we suffered no loss of lives during that terrible storm. But lives weren't the only things lost during Katrina. I along with thousands lost irreplaceable mementos, things that give life so much of its meaning. Leaders in that moment who lacked the will and/or capacity to provide strength through leadership only exacerbated that pain, which still lingers.

For me, this pain was and still is symbolized by a tiny little book that probably meant next to nothing to anyone else on the planet. But it meant the world to me.

My father's father, Walter Morial Sr., was a cigar maker, an amputee, and a man of modest means. He and his wife, Leonie Moore Morial (my grandmother, a seamstress and homemaker), traced their roots back to a free community in Haiti—a Maroon community of blacks who not only talked self-determination but lived it with every breath they took. The Honorable Marcus Mosiah Garvey, the great race leader from Jamaica, traced his roots to a Maroon community in his native land.

My grandmother was a devout Catholic and baked the best cakes you ever wanted to enjoy. One of our family traditions was that she always baked us a cake for our birthdays. Neither my grandmother nor grandfather had much formal education, but both could read and write. They never owned a car and never learned how to drive, but they were principled, hardworking, no-nonsense people whose reputation traveled near and far. As gruff as my grandfather could be, my grandmother was the epitome of being nice, sweet, and caring.

Such communities existed wherever people of African ancestry had been enslaved. Those communities bred in their members a sense of racial pride and dignity that couldn't be faked and would never be given away without bloodshed.

It was out of this fierce sense of pride and nobility—belief that we were so much more than what society said we were—that my grandfather proudly, almost ceremonially, gifted me a book. I can't recall the book's exact title, but I referred to it as *The Little Red Presidents Book*. The assignment from my grandfather: memorize them all. In order. First and last names. And anything else of interest about them. I'm not sure what possessed my young self to embrace this directive, but soon after receiving my orders I completely owned the task.

A few years ago, an old friend reminded me that whenever we went to the barbershop as kids, I would stand atop a soapbox and recite the names of all the presidents—in order—for whoever could stand to listen to me. My love affair with knowledge about the presidents became such an obsession that family members, grandparents, aunts, uncles, cousins, and even folk outside the family would give me books on the presidents for Christmas, birthdays, and other special occasions.

I became so enamored with presidential facts that I began collecting additional books on the topic. I literally had my own presidential library by the time I was a preteen. But none of the books I accumulated on our nation's commanders in chief, no matter their glossy finish or new book smell, ever matched the sentimental significance of that first book given to me by my grandfather.

The Little Red Presidents Book was one of my most prized possessions—one I never planned to let go of. But on August 29, 2005, Hurricane Katrina changed the game. I forever lost that cherished book. But thousands of others lost their own versions of *The Little Red Presidents Book*, their own valued keepsakes.

Hurricane Katrina disrupted and disrespected all that. It was certainly a natural disaster, but it was one made exponentially worse by the human-made disaster of a horrific and unimaginable nonresponse. While our city, truly one of the most unique jewels in all of

America, lay prostrate from the havoc of wind and rain and destroyed levees, the federal government—our federal government—sat back and ignored us, watching as its people literally died in flooded streets. And our local and state leaders sat motionless, with no action whatsoever, staring like a deer in headlights.

If the tragedy of people dying while help was withheld wasn't enough—as if the inhumane conditions of the Superdome-turned-post-apocalyptic scene wasn't enough—a cacophony of national political and media voices declared city residents a group of violent "others" deserving of their plight.

The not-so-subtle inference being made was that New Orleanians were not real citizens, not real Americans. The larger inference being made was that African Americans, and to some degree the nation's poor, were deemed so unworthy that our own government chose to do nothing as disease and despair spread like floodwaters.

And those waters were unforgiving. They rose to damage and take whole houses and structures and neighborhoods. They rose and took lands and parks and lives. They rose and forever washed away cherished heirlooms and items of irreplaceable sentimental value.

New Orleans' criticisms of the grossly inadequate federal response to the Katrina crisis were matched in intensity only by the residents' criticisms about being cast as "refugees." These criticisms led several news organizations to ban the word in their Katrina coverage. Among them were the *Washington Post* and the *Boston Globe*. But others, including the Associated Press and the *New York Times*, continued using the word where they deemed it appropriate.

As I sat in the green room preparing to appear on the September 4, 2005, broadcast of *Meet the Press*, I thought about the disrespectful "refugee" label. I also took in the words of the guests who preceded me on camera. Michael Chertoff, secretary of homeland security and the person in charge of the federal response to the Hurricane Katrina disaster, offered a nonresponse when asked if he and FEMA could have done more for Katrina victims. Show guest Aaron Broussard, president of Jefferson Parish, responded, "The aftermath of

Hurricane Katrina will go down as one of the worst abandonments of Americans on American soil ever in US history."[5]

He added, "It's not just Katrina that caused all these deaths in New Orleans here. Bureaucracy has committed murder here . . . and bureaucracy has to stand trial before Congress now."

Basically, Broussard was condemning the lack of strength coupled with compassion coming from leaders. His words echoed the question I had asked long before arriving on the set of *Meet the Press*.

During those first horrible hours of flooding after the levees burst, when no aid came to New Orleanians, I asked, "Where is the compassion?" As one day of inaction turned into two, then three and four, I asked, "Where is the compassion?" As New Orleans citizens, US citizens, were declared refugees, I asked, "Where is the compassion?"

But I also issued a call for strength—the strength to act and find solutions—and to come together. I called for investments from the private sector and individuals as well as the US government. And my call for coalition and consensus building didn't stop there.

I told the show's host, Tim Russert, "Not only am I upset, shocked, and angry, I hope that as I talk on this show today that this nation will recognize that this is a wake-up call and an opportunity for black and white people to come together to try to do something for the now almost one million people who've been displaced from their homes, unprecedented in American history, a humanitarian crisis of untold proportions. And we've got to focus on that. . . . These are not, Tim, refugees. Let's not refer to them as refugees. They're citizens. They're survivors."

THE COMPASSIONATE JESUIT PRIEST

Many years before Katrina, I saw what strength through compassion looked like close up. While integrating a Christian Brothers

School in New Orleans' City Park and then later attending Jesuit High School, I witnessed this powerful combination through the leadership of Father Harry Tompson.

At Jesuit, there were fourteen black students out of roughly one thousand. One year, we were moved to create a Black History Week display to share with our fellow classmates and teachers the pride we had in our culture. I approached Father Tompson with the idea. To his credit, he was very open and supportive of our idea and suggested we see the librarian for assistance.

Father Tompson also supported our desire to create an organization, the Student Organization of Black Achievement, of which I was the first president while at the same time playing varsity football and basketball.

My interest in black history was piqued as I began to read books that were on my parents' bookshelves. A sampling of these great works includes *The Autobiography of Malcolm X*, Reverend Dr. Martin Luther King Jr.'s *From Chaos to Community*, W. E. B. DuBois's *The Souls of Black Folk,* and so many more.

My brother and I, while youngsters, also discovered a brand-new bookstore called the Ujamaa Market on St. Bernard Avenue in the Seventh Ward, founded by activist and community leader Sekou Fela, who stocked books of black authors, poets, and the like. My brother, Jacques, frequented the Ujamaa Market buying a book here and there. The store contained a treasure trove of material on black history and politics.

While the Ujamaa Market lasted for only a few years, the books I purchased remained on the shelves of my mother's home until they were washed away by Hurricane Katrina. My impetus to start a black history program at my high school was born out of my time reading my parents' books and my time garnering and consuming literary works made available at the Ujamaa Market.

With the librarian's help, we created a really impressive display featuring books, photographs, and quotes that celebrated black people's sojourn in America.

Despite the kudos and positive comments we received from some, however, there were those who were not only unimpressed but angered that black students would dare create such a display. The result: our work was defaced with the letters *KKK* painted over it and KKK literature pasted on top. And, of course, I was called to the principal, Father Tompson's office, along with two other students.

The reason was not to hold us accountable for the vandalism, but rather to direct my advisor and principal on how to move forward. He shared the criticism he'd received from students and some parents for allowing Black History Week to exist.

"They're asking the question 'Why do blacks need their own special week?' What should I tell them?" he asked us. As was my habit, I responded on behalf of all three of us.

"Tell them to organize an Italian History Week and an Irish History Week," I said. "They don't know their own history, and that's why they're mad."

As a teenager I was looking for ways to build coalition, responding out of compassion rather than anger. I looked at things from their perspective and realized ignorance was the real culprit. But my response was also a show of strength—not backing down from our right to celebrate our story and our culture, while offering a solution, an action to address the issue.

I certainly had powerful examples in this regard, including Father Tompson, who became a mentor and close family friend. In response to this racial "controversy," Father Tompson did not lord his position over us but rather compassionately invited us in to discuss ways to confront the situation and move forward.

I went back to my high school a few years ago to help celebrate the fiftieth anniversary of the school's integration. To my surprise, one of my former teachers was still on staff. He told me that the faculty members weren't ready for integration at the time. He said they viewed us simply as brown-skinned whites, not recognizing that we came from different backgrounds and experiences than the school's white students. All they wanted were no incidents.

When I was in school, a faculty member asked me—the only one who was not too afraid ask—why all the black kids always sat together during lunch. In the moment, some fifty years ago, I responded, "All the blacks, musicians, nerds, weed heads sit together—there's stratification in high school that you adults are often unaware of, and race is just one." It was technically an honest answer. But my adult answer during that anniversary fifty years later revealed the heart of the matter: "We sat together because we were in fear of being bullied and called names. And we needed each other's emotional support to survive in a tough, sometimes unwelcoming environment."

Father Tompson's living example of strength and compassion made us feel welcome. It made all the difference in the world. We knew he was genuine and that he cared about our well-being. That's what showing compassion can do—it gets people to buy into you as a human being and welcome you inside their walls of doubt or suspicion. As a leader, compassion moves your team to trust that you have their well-being in mind and that you are willing to see them as human beings—not just cogs in an organization's machine.

Father Tompson also displayed strength. In those challenging years, he gave the black students room to express our ideas and concerns while dealing with the complaints of those who were much less comfortable with our presence at Jesuit. But Father Tompson went a step further. Under his leadership the school hired its first wave of black instructors. He also allowed us black students to actively recruit more black students, a move that effectively tripled the number of black students at Jesuit.

And his strength through compassion didn't stop there. Father Tompson later founded the Good Shepherd School, an academy that primarily served black students. Additionally, he opened a business, Café Reconcile, that gave formerly incarcerated individuals the opportunity for gainful employment. Both institutions he founded still operate and still keep Father Tompson's legacy of strength through compassion alive decades after his passing.

That's what leaders who pair strength with their compassion do—they act with strength and courage to make sure their people have the opportunity to experience positive, winning, and profitable personal and collective outcomes.

I kept in contact with Father Tompson long after my high school days, until he passed away. He took part in my wedding, gave the prayer of invocation when I became mayor, and regularly came over to my home for breakfast. Certainly, not all bosses, organizational heads, elected officials, and leaders of various stripes will have such a personal connection with everyone under their care. But any leader willing to leverage these twin towers of leadership will win at building consensus, collaboration, creativity, and commitment in and from their charges.

GUMBO COALITION RECAP: STRENGTH THROUGH COMPASSION

Showing strength and compassion is not always the most popular thing to do. A leader should be guided by their values and sense of morality.

How do you do that?

Define Your Right Thing—Your right thing should be determined by universally accepted social morals and values.

Do the Right Thing—Inevitably, there will be challenges you face as a leader that test your character and sense of morality. Do the right thing, even if it's not popular and even if you'll get no credit for it.

Know the Effect of Your Affect—As a leader, you must always remember your decisions are not just about you. They impact those you lead.

CHAPTER 5

KNOW WHEN TO HOLD 'EM, KNOW WHEN TO FOLD 'EM

A LEADER IS SKILLED AT DECISION-MAKING UNDER PRESSURE

Every blue moon or so, you'll come upon a pressurized decision-making situation that can literally make or break your reputation. For AT&T CEO Randall Stephenson, that moment came when he rolled the dice and went to court against Uncle Sam.

As the story goes, AT&T sought to purchase Time Warner. The government stepped in and blocked the deal, then entered into protracted negotiations with AT&T to come upon a workable solution. This would involve AT&T giving up a lot of the assets it sought in the initial purchase. If AT&T refused to move forward with the negotiations, the US government promised to sue AT&T.

Now, nine times out of ten, when the US government threatens to sue a company attempting such a business expansion, the company backs down and fully complies with whatever dictates and conditions the government sets. But with Stephenson at the helm, AT&T chose to go to battle in the courts.

To the uninitiated, this move doesn't sound all that daring or bold. But when Stephenson chose to take his case to court, he put not only his reputation as a leader on the line but so much more. If his move failed, which history said it probably would, not only was he in danger of losing his job, but the lost profits would endanger the jobs of many more AT&T employees.

Just read the business section of any paper. CEOs are fired for failed attempts like this. Companies on the losing end of such a battle often take a hit via a dramatic drop in stock prices. Moreover, since he was the head of such a large, iconic, and high-profile corporation, taking on Uncle Sam and losing, already a losing proposition, could have been disastrous for Stephenson's reputation and future prospects.

To say the pressure was on when he weighed his options would be an understatement. For context, AT&T is an American company with a solid record on diversity with African American board members and countless people of color within its ranks, and their diversity programming is formidable. AT&T is the largest multichannel video service provider in the United States by total subscribers. As of 2018, AT&T was ranked number nine on the *Fortune 500* rankings. AT&T generated $170.7 billion in revenue in 2018 and held total assets that year worth $531 billion.

When news broke that Stephenson and AT&T won their case in court and were able to purchase Time Warner without all the initial stipulations, Stephenson looked like a genius. He and his company won even more than they bargained for. It was a great victory. But, believe me, the pressure had been on. His reputation as a leader grew.

For every Stephenson victory, however, there are countless defeats, lost profits, and derailed careers.

COMPETITIVE TOUR BECOMES PROTECTIVE TOUR

With Stephenson and AT&T, the safety and security of entire cities were not in jeopardy. I, however, had faced the challenge of protecting cities. And it all began during the course of a long-awaited and highly anticipated meeting for which I invested countless hours preparing. But with what transpired that day, nothing could have fully prepared me.

Meeting day had finally come, September 11, 2001. Tom Cochran, executive director of the United States Conference of Mayors, and I arrived early at our destination, the Willard Hotel in our nation's capital. After being escorted to our conference room, Cochran and I, along with Michael Deaver, our PR consultant, sat reviewing our pitch, waiting for David Broder, a columnist with the *Washington Post*. Once he arrived, we launched into explaining our Competitive Cities Tour, highlighting the incredible job mayors had done throughout the nation to lead their cities toward a renaissance of lowered crime rates and higher positive outcomes.

As I mentioned before, the Clinton administration with the leadership of the HUD secretary demonstrated a welcomed passion to assist mayors after the years of cold neglect of the Reagan and George H.W. Bush years, when they sought to cut funding to cities. In the late 1990s, American business began to awaken to the new opportunities and to look anew to American cities as places to invest, just as a housing renaissance began.

With George W. Bush (Bush 43) now in the White House, we worried that the Clinton-era enthusiasm to support mayors would fade. Though White House support for the frontline work of mayors did not dip nearly as much as we feared, the media in the late 1990s shamefully underreported this powerful development of the successes of urban areas. So, as leaders of an organization representing mayors across the country, we were bursting at the seams, ready to unveil our campaign that would draw a much-deserved spotlight on the comeback of urban areas.

Our campaign, called the Competitive Cities Tour, ironically, was being shaped with the counsel of Michael Deaver, who was the message maestro for President Ronald Reagan. Our tour was also directed at the new administration of President George W.

Bush to encourage continuation of the Clinton-era emphasis on American cities.

But before we could really get rolling, my communications director interrupted the meeting to inform us that a plane had tragically flown off course and crashed into one of the towers of New York's World Trade Center. Moments later, she burst into the room alerting us that the crash was no accident and that a second plane had barreled into the other tower.

At this point members of federal security escorted us from the building to a secure site reserved for elected officials. The drive there was harrowing and surreal. We sped up and down streets and sidewalks, any space the driver could find, as people were literally running in the streets in a panic.

Once we made it safely to our destination through what seemed a post-apocalyptic scene, the two of us were ordered to hunker down, along with Anthony Williams, mayor of Washington, DC, until movement was deemed safe. We were there in that space for nearly five hours, the presentation for our Competitive Cities Tour still in hand.

What Cochran and I both knew instinctively was that our plan made no sense given the reality unfolding around us. It didn't matter the hours of planning and preplanning that had gone into its formation. It didn't matter that all the elements of securing a fast start had been built in. It didn't matter that powerful leadership principles had been integrated throughout and that strength and compassion were evidenced in numerous ways.

We knew that, as leaders of major cities, frontline champions expected to make things happen, we needed a new plan immediately. As the nightmare of 9/11 was still unfolding around us, no amount of our personal fear and angst would change the fact that we needed a totally new plan, one that provided cities with very real safety and security from very real threats of terrorist violence.

Leaders with any level of experience know that a major part of planning and execution is making necessary adjustments as challenges and unforeseen issues arise. Ironically, surprises are to be expected, and leaders who so stubbornly refuse to make these minor adjustments often find their best-laid plans going astray.

This was not the case for Cochran and me that day. This was not one of those moments calling for minor adjustments to our original vision. No. As painful as it was, the only strong move, the only compassionate move, was to throw out our Competitive Cities Tour entirely and devise a new plan that met the dire challenges of our newfound reality. Like the lyrics of the Kenny Rogers classic "The Gambler" says, "You've got to know when to hold 'em, know when to fold 'em." If we were to be responsible leaders, we had to fold 'em and create a new vision, a new plan. We had to take a different path than Randall Stephenson.

Being able to create something new demands that you not remain enslaved to your old plan, no matter how fantastic or dynamic it was. That Competitive Cities Tour, I am certain, would have been the talk of the nation. It would have shone the spotlight on some very deserving individuals and initiatives nationwide that had been lost in a sea of negative media coverage. That Competitive Cities Tour would have been a game changer, shifting the conversation about the value and importance of cities from our failures and onto our successes. But had I been enslaved to that Competitive Cities Tour amid America's new post-9/11 reality, not only would I have been laughed out of town, hundreds of thousands, if not millions, of American citizens would have been far less safe, far less secure.

Time was of the essence. Even as the horrible events of the day were still unfolding, Cochran and I got to work in our bunker devising a plan for the nation's mayors to push for safety measures to meet the needs of a shaken people. I argued that mayors run airports because cities own airports, and since America's largest city was the one attacked, every city is therefore at risk. So mayors must lead the response. Here I was, the leader of America's mayors, and it was time to act.

In that room, I surmised that Americans would want federalized screeners at airports and other transportation points. The show of a safety force was critical. This idea and others were presented to a special session of the United States Conference of Mayors just thirty days later. It was a summit to flesh out in full our plan for the safety of American cities—the brand-new plan born in that bunker on 9/11 to replace our original one.

We were going to show how cities were coming back. But with the felled Twin Towers, we had to devise a plan for cities that reflected the reality that US cities were not exempt from the dangers of the world.

In fact, even before that gathering in mid-October, at DC's Capital Hilton Hotel just days after 9/11, I had called for an emergency meeting.[1] Present at that emergency meeting were police and fire chiefs, mayors, and other city officials, along with paramedics from across the country. Through extensive meetings that day and subsequent meetings thereafter, this national coalition created recommendations we believed would best meet the needs of our national citizenry. In essence, we were going to lobby Washington to create one unified top security agency.

And that's exactly what we did. This diverse coalition of leaders took the bold step in the wake of the September 11 terrorist attacks to request that Congress create a new department with the mission of providing adequate security for our national "homeland." This emergency gathering of mayors, with critical input from first responders, called for the formation of the Department of Homeland Security. This was before President Bush decided to support the creation of this department.

For Cochran and me, the pressure to create a viable national security plan was immediate and monumental. For all members of the United States Conference of Mayors, the pressure existed to create something tangible to offer citizens of our respective cities, something that provided the safety and security the entire nation needed. Theoretically, folding under pressure was a possibility, but it was a luxury we couldn't afford.

Decision-making under pressure is one of the requirements for the job of leader. Pressure is going to come one way or another. In fact, most times, pressure comes from multiple directions—sometimes in stages, but often all at once. A leader must realize it's not a matter of if but when those pressure-filled moments are going to arise. As a leader you must be able to keep your head and make those critical, often time-sensitive decisions when everything in the world seems to be riding on the course you chart for your citizens, your employees, everyone. You can't be guided by anger, revenge, or fear. These things get you off your game. That's why being emotionally grounded is one of the most important yet underrated attributes of an effective leader.

Being sensitive to the realities around you and the needs of your constituents or customers is key to making decisions under pressure. Entrepreneurs probably know this best. When running a small business, you're essentially running everything—marketing, accounting, maintenance, and office management. That's the ultimate pressure. But again, leaders of all stripes will face those moments when they are forced to make decisions under less than ideal circumstances.

And that's what brings about much of the pressure. It's not only the magnitude of the decision but the lack of time you have to make it. In that 9/11 bunker, we didn't have the luxury of time or the luxury of reflection, which just added to the pressure of the moment. We had to make quick decisions about how to best lead mayors and lead cities.

The whole episode reminds me of one of my favorite sayings: "Diamonds are made under pressure." I believe leaders, real leaders, thrive under pressure. Sure, there are tons of negatives associated with pressure. But it can bring out the best in you if you can keep your head. It can sharpen your focus on what's most important and help you bypass everything else. It can heighten your own sense of urgency. Pressure can push you past the "paralysis of analysis" so you're not wasting time contemplating for three hours or three days the same decision you were ready to make in the first three minutes. If you let it, pressure can bring out the best in you.

The other side of pressure, though, is that it can impact your decisions and thus the effect they have on others and on your own reputation. My moment to face this reality and place my reputation on the line came as a newly elected mayor choosing my new police chief.

As I mentioned earlier, I bypassed the police chief search committee to choose the person I wanted to hire. That move could have gone horribly wrong. Crime was the number one issue in New Orleans at the time. All the hype and all the news were about New Orleans' crime and what leader could do something about it.

Moreover, I ran on being able to do something about it. Had the person I hired for the job been a bust, it would have been game over for me. I easily could have been labeled a failed mayor in my first few months, making it almost impossible to build momentum, trust, goodwill, and consensus. As it turned out, that hire was probably one of my best ever. Richard Pennington, who served me for eight years as New Orleans Police Chief, became my partner, and one of the best police chiefs in the nation during the '90s. The entire situation was pressure packed, and I didn't help matters any. In fact, I added to the pressure of the decision by going outside the process.

Luckily you can develop the skills to make good decisions under pressure. Make it simple. Take out a sheet of paper and go old school—write a list of pros and cons. If you have multiple options, list the pros and cons for both.

Also, consult with your team—and not just any group of top executives. Rather, invite your most trusted allies, friends, and advisors to offer their input. Just remember, you will still have to make the ultimate decision yourself.

Scenario playing also helps; envision how your city, school, or business might look thirty, sixty, or ninety days out after your decision. But nothing tops putting in the work of preparation. Doing my homework has been essential to every major decision I've ever made.

BETTING ON RESPECT

One of the most controversial issues that came my way as New Orleans' mayor was the construction of the New Orleans Casino. This was the part of that first leg of attempts to expand legalized gambling outside of Las Vegas. And selling it to New Orleanians was not easy. Personally, I don't like gambling and I don't gamble. But I really loved the idea of a bill that would bring my city twenty-two hundred jobs, each paying living and middle-class wages with solid benefits.

What made the casino so controversial was the fact that local evangelical Christians were dead set against it. They regularly packed the capital building in protest. Mainline business also opposed it. This was a coalition rarely seen. The *Times-Picayune* also railed against it.

Additionally, operators of New Orleans' dynamic and pervasive church bingo operations viewed the bill as a threat. And they were right to do so. The church bingo scene had a huge political component. All candidates had to do was make a contribution to the bingo pot and they were given the mic, free to address potential voters face-to-face. When it eventually passed, the bill all but put church bingo out of business.

Many of the city's hotel owners were leery of the casino project and insisted that casino developers be prevented from building hotel rooms, a decision that was reversed many years later.

Another casualty was the vast network of community-level gambling, street corner bookies, and the like. That was a community-level system and dynamic I appreciated. It was so New Orleans. But within this context—the potential loss of community institutions, the pushback from huge groups with real voting power—I had a decision to make. And it was one that brought me full circle in my political career.

When the bill was first introduced, I was a member of the Louisiana State Senate. There I took the position that if gambling was to come to New Orleans, its citizens should have the right to vote on it themselves. Hence, I promised to vote no on the bill. That stance angered both the then mayor and the governor. The pressure on me was real. I had several people of real power and stature pushing me to go one way, while I was determined, based on principle, to go another. When the bill came up for vote, I kept my word and voted no after sponsoring an amendment to require a vote of the people of New Orleans before the casino could open. My amendment failed by one vote. Had my amendment passed, I would have voted yes.

But when I became mayor of New Orleans, the casino that had been the cause of so much pressure and focus when I was a state senator filed for bankruptcy. Before the bankruptcy filing, I had a celebrated showdown with then governor Edwin Edwards. It became a classic example of when to hold 'em.

At the time, the casino was preparing to open in a temporary location, but I knew that the state had not agreed to reimburse the city for its fair share of city services as required by the casino law. I decided to hold up the casino opening by refusing to give a permit to open until an agreement had been reached and funds delivered. This angered Edwards and his allies, which were many.

Though I had not been close to Edwards, I supported his reelection in 1991. Nonetheless, Edwards accused me of holding up jobs. I accused him of not being fair to a city that had been the base of his reelection.

I calculated that the city would be left holding the bag with no money if we allowed the casino to open before the state agreed to pay us the money that state law mandated. In this instance, I drew the line in the sand. Now, it must be stated that I was sixty days into my first term as mayor. As such, many considered my taking on the most powerful politician in the state (and a fellow Democrat) so openly and brazenly to be a foolhardy move.

Edwards was a reasonable man in most circumstances. I knew he was so committed to the casino that he would eventually yield to our demands. But I knew he would not do so without a fight. So I set up a meeting with Edwards on his turf.

With me for this meeting were members of the New Orleans legislative delegation and city council members. Our goal was to iron things out with the governor in his place of comfort, the governor's mansion.

As we walked in, the media was surrounding the mansion waiting for the outcome of the meeting. By any and all measures, the meeting did not go well. Edwards walked into the meeting and in a threatening way challenged what I had done. After he vented for five to seven minutes, I stood up and said the city of New Orleans would not concede to any of his demands without precondition. At that point, the meeting was over. We had a public standoff.

When we exited the meeting, it was 2:00 p.m., and as Baton Rouge was only ninety minutes away from New Orleans, we had just enough time to call a press conference for the top of the news cycle. I decided then to go back to New Orleans and hold a press conference, which was covered by every station in the city. I announced as if speaking directly to Governor Edwards, yet speaking to his and my own constituents, that the ball was in the governor's court and that he should do the right thing and give us the money. I resisted any urge to personally criticize Edwards as I knew that he was savvy and experienced enough to understand the chess move I had made.

That move must have been effective because Edwards immediately deployed Bill Broadhurst, one of his closest confidants and a very talented lawyer in his own right, to begin negotiations with

Bob Tucker, who handled negotiations on my behalf. After several days of intense, behind-the-scenes negotiation, I was able to announce a deal totaling $22 million to support the city over the next several years. In this instance I was called to take a tough stance even against an ally, to stand up for my city, and to reestablish the position of the New Orleans mayor's office as a position of power, leadership, and toughness.

A few months after the casino project opened, it applied for bankruptcy protection.

Thus a city vote was eventually needed if casino gambling was to come to New Orleans. This issue had come full circle. And once again all those local pressures rose as one.

Yet the city's economy was starving for employment opportunities. Casino gambling would provide just that. I had several irate citizens meet with me, imploring me to oppose the casino. My response to them was that, though I am personally not enamored with gambling, I can't turn my back on two thousand–plus well-paying jobs. I challenged them to provide me with another option that could provide the city with that many jobs at that rate of pay. No one could.

Still, the majority of citizens agreed with my position. But in saying that, it grossly underplays the level of pressure that I lived with daily through that entire process. I had nearly as many constituents standing against me as I did standing with me. But when you assume the mantle of leadership, those moments will arise, those difficult moments that will leave you feeling uneasy. You're going to have to take stances that many will oppose. The real pressure comes in staying true to your conscience. I firmly believed that the good outweighed the bad when it came to gambling in New Orleans. It was certainly neither an easy nor a comfortable position to take. However, I believed it to be the position that would best serve my city.

And it's decisions like that, pressure-filled, often unpopular decisions, that leaders have to be prepared to make. Staff layoffs, business relocations, termination of entire product lines, the introduction of new ones, the elimination of sports programs at a university due to financial challenges—decisions like these invite opposition. And with opposition will most certainly come pressure.

GUMBO COALITION RECAP: DECISION MAKING UNDER PRESSURE

Be a Healthy Skeptic, Not a Cynic or Bottleneck—A skeptic trusts but verifies. A cynic distrusts everything. A bottleneck believes they must review everything in detail. You can't be a rubber-stamp manager. You have to trust but verify, even with your own people. You have to question, taking in all the information, and make decisions quickly about everything you have verified.

No Textbook Management—Avoid blindly delegating and then going into your Rip Van Winkle routine. What I mean by that is don't delegate and disappear. You've got to check in. I have tons of five-minute meetings and two-minute phone calls just to check in. Stay looped in. Use technology effectively. Technology has enabled more frequent and ease of communication. Take advantage of it.

CHAPTER 6

GET READY FOR THE BIG PAYBACK

A LEADER IS NOT PARALYZED BY THE UNEXPECTED

The dead body with a bullet through the heart, found at the corner of Chartres Street and Elysian Fields Avenue, on the morning of October 11, 1998, was that of Raymond Myles. At the time of his death, Myles was considered a local gospel legend. To me, however, his death wasn't the loss of a recording artist but the loss of a friend. Myles's death ignited a fire in me that in turn set off a firestorm I never saw coming. Eradicating gun violence had been an obsession of mine since childhood.

Myles's death compelled me to recall the death of my childhood friend, Donald Spraul. He was my best friend in first and second grade even though the two of us lived on opposite sides of the ditch that separated Pontchartrain Park (the black neighborhood) and Gentilly Woods (the white neighborhood). I must mention that Donald was white. For the pair of us on different sides of the ditch to become friends was quite rare in those days. We spent countless days hanging out at each other's homes, building our friendship. So when I received the news as a ten year-old that my friend Donald was shot and killed, I felt that loss deeply. Though Don wasn't killed through violence—he was killed in a freak hunting accident—in my mind, Don's death registered as yet another example of why I view gun violence with disdain.

At the time of Myles's death, I was part of a US Conference of Mayors' Task Force that was in negotiations with the NRA and the Gun Manufacturers Association of America (GMAA).

This ad hoc task force's negotiations aimed to find a win-win scenario. By that, I mean a scenario that would allow American cities to enact policies that would drastically reduce the number of guns that find their way to our streets while honoring Second Amendment protections and the gun companies' rights to make a profit. Although some of my fellow mayors took the NRA and GMAA representatives at their word, I never thought they were negotiating in good faith. Unfortunately, I was correct.

The task force was still in the midst of those "road-to-nowhere" negotiations when my friend Raymond Myles was stricken down by a gun's bullet. Just a few weeks before, Myles performed at the inauguration festivities marking my second term. Now he was another gun violence statistic. The contingent of mayors stressed staying the course, but frankly, I had had enough. I broke ranks, stepped out on my own, and sued the NRA and GMAA, holding them responsible for the rash of gun violence murders suffocating the country.

My fellow mayors were pissed to put it lightly. I remember Philadelphia's mayor, Ed Rendell, calling to discourage me from not staying in lockstep with the other mayors. I certainly understood his position, but as I explained to him, my local politics, my city, and my personal connection with Myles took precedence.

Twenty days after Myles's body was found, I stood in my office on Halloween Day 1998, wearing a jack-o'-lantern tie and holding a press conference to announce the lawsuit. Our lead lawyer was Wendell Gauthier, one of the lead counsel in the successful class action lawsuits against the tobacco industry. I can't say that my actions set off a chain reaction, but the very next day the city of Chicago announced a similar lawsuit. Eventually thirty-five cities in all sued the NRA and their primary financial backers in what was now a national campaign to halt the Wild West–style proliferation of guns.

The move made national news, and our office enjoyed overwhelming support from New Orleanians tired of the violence. I surely knew that the NRA would counter with some nasty words about me or send another gentleman with a big briefcase and a bigger checkbook authorized to buy as much public opinion for their side as possible, as they had done in the past. But what I did not see coming was the ferocity, the multitiered attacks, the big guns pulled out to attack every fiber of my political, professional, and personal being.

The moves the NRA made were almost overwhelming in their breadth and scope. They took me by surprise. They refused to blow it off or take it lightly. They were coming with the big payback.

The NRA forces attacked me personally and politically. One of their tactics involved a misinformation campaign to turn public opinion against me. Before the lawsuit, the New Orleans Police Department did a highly publicized gun swap—trading old police weapons for upgraded Glock 9 weapons for our police force—for every gun they turned into authorities. This program worked great and other municipalities used it often. But with misinformation, the NRA flipped the script. They accused us of allowing swapped firearms to be purposefully dumped back onto the streets—more specifically, to the city's criminals.

They also threatened to boycott the city's hospitality industry by moving a previously scheduled national convention out of New Orleans if we didn't drop the lawsuit. I knew this was a bluff because convention contracts had already been signed. The NRA contingent would not be willing to take that financial and potential legal hit. But their announced boycott did achieve part of its objective. It turned many of the city's hospitality workers and business owners against the lawsuit simply out of self-preservation.

The NRA, however, still wasn't done.[1]

They deployed the biggest gun of all, actor Charlton Heston, to further their attacks. Before becoming the NRA's official national spokesman, Heston was one of the most legendary movie stars Hollywood ever produced. His list of edgy, groundbreaking movies is phenomenal, but it was his role as Moses in the iconic movie *The Ten Commandments* that elevated him far above mere mortal actors. So to say I was blindsided by the appearance of "Moses" arriving on the scene to be the official NRA mouthpiece attacking me, my integrity, the lawsuit, and thus my city would be a gross understatement. There I was, the mayor of a city, fighting against a Hollywood icon who was not only Moses, but Ben-Hur and the guy who took on the Planet of the Apes by himself.

When I filed that lawsuit, I knew the NRA would make some noise, but I did not foresee national-level blowback. I would have never guessed they would misrepresent a gun swap. I was nowhere near as ready as I should have been. As a result, I had to make up a plan on the fly.

That plan centered on very public debates with NRA representatives. That way, I could maximize one of my key strengths—my ability to argue a case and persuade individuals to buy into my position. The debates helped push back against the NRA's coordinated PR campaign, but we were still fighting an uphill battle.

As a result of those debates I gained thousands of haters nationally. The attention rattled members of New Orleans' hospitality industry even more. But we were still able to gain ground on the strength of a powerful counter message that focused on the lawsuit's main goal—increased safety for citizens.

Believe me, I heard the NRA company line at each debate—guns don't kill people, people kill people. My response: people with guns kill people. How do I know? Because we don't have an epidemic of strangulation deaths, but we do have a rash of gun deaths.

From this on-the-fly plan, we were ultimately able to gain our footing and fight the NRA team in court. They were slick, however, and worked by supporting elected officials to create a law undermining and disabling our lawsuit. The case went all the way to the Louisiana Supreme Court. And though we lost, I did not regret the fight. It was the principle that moved me to do the lawsuit, not policy. Had I been all about policy, the focus would have been on rhetoric rather than action.

What I did regret was not being fully ready for the big payback. As I said, surprises are a natural part of life, business, and leadership. That doesn't mean you can prepare for all possibilities, but it does mean there are steps you can take to minimize the negative impact of surprises.

I have been asked, if I had this chapter of my life to do all over again, would I still bring that lawsuit. My answer: yes, without question or hesitation. The lawsuit was filed during a period in this nation's history when gun violence was rampant. It was an issue mayors were discussing and taking up all over the country. Those mayors were all saying the same thing—we've got to do something about this violence ravaging our cities, about these military weapons with rapid-fire capacity setting up whole communities for slaughter.

Almost prophetically, our lawsuit occurred a few months before the tragic mass shooting at Columbine High School.

If I had this chapter to do over, I would still file that lawsuit. But this time I would do so realizing that, when you challenge the status quo, the counterpunch will be absolutely ferocious. And punches will come from all angles. I would make anticipating and countering those blows part of my planning process.

I would employ a planning device I had used hundreds if not thousands of times before and since—playing out multiple scenarios. Scenario playing is the essence of collaborative thinking. Figuring out how things play out before making a decision is not something that can be done in your head alone. You need diverse thought and ideas that come with engaging the energies of others, when everyone in the room is asking and answering the questions "If we do X, what move are they going to make? And if that's their response, how do we respond?"

As a leader of a business, school, or organization, you may not have the full weight of an entire industry and their lobbying firm come down on your head, but you will face a circumstance or two that come out of nowhere and hits you in the gut. Hard.

When that happens, what do you do?

First, you switch to catch-up mode. You've been blindsided and need to regain your bearings. You may have to take a step back and evaluate the best response under the circumstance. This means considering a few things: Is the hit you've taken temporary or long-standing? How strong or weak is your opponent? What is the most appropriate timing for your response, meaning should it be immediate or will it be most effective if you take your time?

With Myles's murder, I knew I had to act fast.

At the age of five, Myles started performing, singing with his mother at local churches. By the time he was twelve, he already had a local gospel hit playing on the radio, "Prayer From a Twelve-Year-Old Boy." From there, his career continued to skyrocket. He became a regular performer at the vaunted New Orleans Jazz and Heritage Festival. The festival's founder, George Wein, called Myles "a monster artist, piano player, arranger, singer—one of the greatest ever from New Orleans." And certainly, that's saying something.

Myles was also beloved as a public-school teacher who coached and counseled local youth. Yet he was able to juggle that work with his growing career, which took him in 1992 all the way to Madison Square Garden, opening for fellow New Orleanian Harry Connick Jr. But Connick was not the only national star to recognize Myles's gifts. Al Green, Patti LaBelle, and the late, great Aretha Franklin each had Myles performing with them at various points.

This budding star, known locally as Maestro, was born the same year as I was—1958. Though we didn't meet until we were teenagers, from that first encounter we remained lifelong friends. So when I got word that this close friend had been taken by gun violence, when I witnessed an entire city go into mourning over his murder, I knew I had to act.

And when I moved to act, I did so with a doubly heavy heart. For Myles's death reminded me of my other close friend's death where a gun was involved.

For me, the issue of gun control was about keeping good people like Donald Spraul and Raymond Myles out of harm's way. And my perspective on the issue may have added to the blindside of the NRA's big payback. They weren't looking at this issue from my very personal perspective.

In middle school, I wrote a paper titled "Weaponsmania" about the hysteria of gun violence and proliferation of guns nationally. Remarkably, this was years before such weapons were as readily available as they are today. However, the rash of major assassinations nationally that occurred during the late '60s and early '70s still weighed heavily upon me. The violent gun murders of Malcolm X, Dr. Martin Luther King Jr., President John F. Kennedy, Medgar Evers, Fred Hampton, Bobby Hutton, the students at Kent State University, and others impacted me personally.

These deaths were the main topics of conversation in the Morial household—conversations involving my parents and the bevy of lawyers, NAACP and National Urban League members, and others who frequently visited. These conversations impacted not only their political leanings and worldviews but mine as well. And as a child, it all seemed so simplistic—unfettered access to guns equaled the violent deaths of far too many. I saw little to no redeeming value in what seemed to be a gun-crazy culture gone wild. I had ample proof of my position coming from every corner of the country.

But Donald's death brought that reality even closer to home. Years later, Myles's death did the same. If I had this chapter of my life to do over, I would know not to simply think about my first move, but also the second, third, and fourth. You can't wait to get hit before you start attempting to put a strategy together.

In hindsight, I would have developed a national PR plan to counter the national PR efforts to undermine our lawsuit. In other words, I would have given more time and attention to overcommunicating my position. I also would have spent more time building community support, including support from law enforcement, the economic sector, and civic organizations, to counter the boycott threats—investing more energy into aligning all the necessary resources for success.

I would have had my playbook of scenarios at the ready with moves and countermoves already outlined and primed to go into motion. I would have been ready to execute my plan to the full.

In business, no matter how good you think your product is, competitors are out there trying to take you down, devising schemes and surprises to throw you and your product off your game. Scenario playing is just as critical for a business leader as it is for the mayor of a city. Through scenario playing you may realize those areas of your operation that need to get stronger. You may find blind spots in your operation you never noticed.

Scenario playing is a powerful tool—as is reflection.

Reflection is critical for a leader. Reflection generally takes place during those post-event review sessions. But the person striving to be a transformational leader reflects regularly. Reflecting on the NRA experience revealed that in that instance I didn't follow my own guide, my own advice, or my own success formula.

The citywide public safety plan my team introduced upon taking office involved various scenarios. These discussions revealed that our plan had to include buy-in from a wide array of constituents. These discussions revealed that our plan could not fall into the old liberal versus conservative rhetoric trap that would place us in one box or another. We knew our safety plan had to not only be framed in language that spoke to both camps but provide nuts-and-bolts offerings that met social services needs as well law-and-order objectives.

These discussions revealed that misinformation could be our ruin. As a result, our prep for those potential surprises allowed us to set up briefings with various constituent groups immediately after the press conference announcing the plan. We rolled out the plan at

11:00 a.m., then held back-to-back briefings on the hour with business leaders, religious leaders, members of the black press, members of the traditional press, education leaders, and others.

Leaders make their names and define their legacies by how well they deal with surprises. Planning in a way that addresses as many scenarios as possible won't guarantee that you will anticipate every eventuality, but it will give you the advanced playbook you need to see your way through any challenge.

THE MASTER OF ANTICIPATION

As I prepared to file suit against the NRA and the gun manufacturers, I wish I had recalled one of my early life lessons of not being caught off guard, a lesson I learned early in life from Mr. Price. Mr. Price was a master of anticipation and the head custodian and building manager at the Knights of Peter Claver Building, where my father's law office was located.

Besides spending many days and hours at the State Capitol Building, my father and I were also regularly in New Orleans' Knights of Peter Claver Building. The building was ground zero for New Orleans' movers and shakers of color. The local NAACP and Urban League chapters had offices there, as did countless other progressive organizations, black businesses, and black attorneys. It was like Howard University and Harlem all rolled into one.

While my father worked, I befriended Mr. Price. I'm not sure if I ever knew Mr. Price's first name, as in those days, children never dared address an adult in such a casual manner. But what I did know, and what everyone who spent any time in that building knew, was that Mr. Price was the most dapper, clean, well-dressed custodian the world had ever known. He came to work the picture of regality and style and left for home the same way—casket sharp.

But it was not only Mr. Price's stylish dress that made him *GQ* smooth. Daily, he drove what had to be the cleanest ride in the parking lot—a snow-white, fin-tailed Cadillac. The care and attention to detail Mr. Price obviously invested in his work was evidenced daily, relentlessly, consistently in his tasks as the Knights of Peter Claver Building's lead custodian.

One of those tasks involved buffing and shining the floor of the rotunda, the main entranceway for all who entered the building. I have no idea where this task ranked on Mr. Price's list of daily duties, but from what I regularly witnessed, he treated it as if it were his most important. And for this critical task, Mr. Price pulled out all the stops. He not only used his strict, step-by-step process for maximizing the shine, he applied his special, secret formula floor wax that transformed a simple floor into mirrorlike magnificence.

A word about the incomparable Mr. Price. Every day I stopped by his office he would ask me to read the sports page out loud, which I did gladly. Each day he would protest and complain about the fact that he forgot his glasses at home and that his failing eyes would not allow him to read those small printed words himself. Hence, he needed my assistance and the power of my youthful vision.

I noticed on more than one occasion that, even though he would say he left his glasses at home, they were right there on his desk. It dawned on me later that Mr. Price either had difficulty reading or he couldn't read at all. For my part, I read with all the vigor I could muster, pretending each moment that I was a sports announcer, reading out loud the latest-breaking sports news as if I were on camera, reading the same way I read out loud in class.

This experience helped me always be clued into people's vulnerabilities. I began to recognize how people regularly made moves to protect these vulnerable parts of themselves. Mr. Price didn't want me to know about his issue, so he took steps to camouflage it as best he could. In this sense, Mr. Price was and is far from being alone. And a leader notices such actions and makes moves to honor the person's vulnerabilities or help them move beyond their shame in the most compassionate way possible. Both responses are examples of strength through compassion.

Notwithstanding Mr. Price's reading challenges, he was most certainly a man of great wisdom, and I to this day consider him a great mentor.

I somehow convinced Mr. Price to share his secret formula with me for my first entrepreneurial venture, Mercury Janitorial Service, founded when I was fifteen with two childhood friends. Mr. Price's liquid shine, however, wasn't the most valuable thing I took from our time together. Every day, like clockwork, Mr. Price would just be finishing up buffing and waxing the building's main entranceway when his boss would arrive. Every day, like clockwork, the two distinguished gentlemen would exchange greetings. Every day, like clockwork, the big boss would comment on how incredible the floors shined, becoming a work of art all its own. I often wondered how this interaction took place so consistently, without fail.

"I know exactly when my boss will arrive, so I make sure to be there in the rotunda so that he can see the work, the effort, I put into my job," he said. The lesson: there's no shame in actively marketing yourself and your work. Proudly and boldly make sure that people, especially bosses, know without a doubt the incredible effort you invest in your work.

I dare say, Mr. Price was never, ever surprised by his boss's arrival. He took incredible measures to avoid being blindsided. How amazing life would be if we could take such steps to guarantee never being surprised in our business ventures or leadership efforts. But such is not the case.

In fact, one of the most powerful constants in all of life, business or otherwise, is the fact that surprises are the most predictable part of life, especially for leaders. One of the most important leadership skills to have in your repertoire is knowing how to navigate those unexpected twists and turns. And we've all had them. The longtime client who suddenly jumps ship. The guaranteed successful product or initiative that tanks. The secondary or tertiary initiative that experiences viral appeal. Harsh and possibly deserved criticism for an advertisement viewed as insensitive or disrespectful to a large segment of society.

The ability to deal with surprises, then, is often the dividing line separating the good and average leaders from those who are exceptional, those who become transformational.

I certainly wish I'd had Mr. Price's superpower to stave off surprises when I took on the NRA and gun manufacturers as a state senator and later as New Orleans' mayor. However, the lessons I learned from that experience, and from Mr. Price's dogged commitment to preparedness, have allowed me to grow and become a more effective leader.

GUMBO COALITION RECAP: DEALING WITH SURPRISE

Scenario Exercises—Anticipate the reaction of other parties to a transaction, whether it be your allies, competitors, or opponents.

a) Competitors—Coke versus Pepsi

b) Opponents—The United States and China imposing tariffs on each other

Plan your second move before you make your first. Make your moves with careful consideration, anticipating the reaction.

Develop a best-practices response plan for human-made or natural disasters, for example, hurricanes, forest fires, mass shootings, terrorist attacks, and so on.

SECTION THREE

THE DITCH

As I mentioned earlier, a ditch, or narrow drainage canal, that filled up only in times of New Orleans' heavy rains separated my neighborhood, the all-black Pontchartrain Park, from the all-white Gentilly Woods neighborhood. I crossed that ditch many a day to visit my friend Donald Spraul as well as to get to and from elementary school. Two other black boys and I were among the few that integrated the all-white elementary school on the other side of that ditch. We were elementary school kids who would learn quickly about our racial differences.

We were often chased as we walked home by older, bigger white kids who called us everything but a child of God. We never told our parents that our hearts raced at the end of every school day, not knowing if that particular journey home would involve another n-word-laden run for our lives or a rare break from the torment. I crossed that ditch daily and have honestly never stopped.

That ditch became the defining symbol of my life. After elementary school, I attended Christian Brothers School, a prestigious middle school in City Park. Even though I no longer had to physically cross it, the ditch reality—the wrestling with life in two different worlds—was in full effect.

Christian Brothers School was located in an old mansion owned by Texas oil baron and millionaire William McFadden. It was a beautiful setting with luscious grass lawns, sunken gardens, a large marble-lined indoor swimming pool, and much more. This incredible edifice became Christian Brothers School, run by Christian Brothers, an order of classic religious teachers. Many of the brothers were from families of New Mexico and Texas. Several were of Hispanic origin and came from modest families. They were great teachers and compassionate men.

Pontchartrain Park was an incredible place to grow up. It comprised aspiring African American families, teachers, truck drivers, musicians, doctors, lawyers, and lots of veterans taking advantage of VA-insured mortgages. However, the world I stepped into at Christian Brothers School may as well have been of another planet.

First of all, alone I represented 50 percent of the school's entire black population. My classmates' parents weren't the truck drivers and lawyers and teachers I knew. They were considered New Orleans' upper crust: the owners of the trucking companies and partners in the law firms that Pontchartrain Park parents often worked for. They were the board members of major corporations and historic churches, prominent figures in the Mardi Gras organizations' inner circle, and card-carrying members of the country club set. As the old-timers from my neighborhood would say, I was in high cotton.

More specifically, I was in the gifted and talented program of a very demanding school that challenged us with essentially a "double-skip" curriculum—a workload that was two years beyond our current grade levels. The academically accelerated pace definitely changed my life, as did the daily exposure and peeks into a world far different from mine. Every day at Christian Brothers School I was living a ditch existence—mastering the spaces between two worlds, while getting more comfortable operating in both.

To get there, beginning as a ten-year-old fifth grader, I started riding the city's public transportation system, meaning I took three buses, transferring twice. I was becoming extremely independent—simultaneously, my athletic prowess grew as fast as my academic advancements. In seventh grade, I made the citywide all-star football and basketball teams, the latter of which practiced in the Ninth Ward, a predominantly black section of town considered New Orleans' most impoverished. This meant crossing multiple "ditches" daily, leaving my neighborhood at the crack of dawn heading to school, and then after the last bell hopping on multiple buses to head to the historic Ninth—the same section of the city that a quarter of a century later would be the hardest hit by Hurricane Katrina. There, I encountered another fellowship—some of the city's top athletes, black and white. Through our rigorous work on the basketball court, I saw and experienced different worlds coming together.

But I also experienced the clash of cultures, such as when our history class grappled with lessons on the Civil War. These lessons, guided by some of the most gifted educators I ever encountered, were thorough and dynamic, engaging us fully—so much so that, during and between classes, students would talk about the various aspects of the Civil War.

The conversation I remember most came when several classmates declared they were openly rooting for the South to win the war—as if it were being fought in our lifetime. When they asked, I quite understandably told them I sided with the North. Their lack of understanding of my position spoke volumes about the differences that openly existed between what I considered my world and theirs.

The ditch always seemed to find a way to make its presence felt. And high school was no different. As an athlete, I found myself in a different world, the stereotypically anti-athlete world—the nerd world—while attending my daily honors classes. There weren't a lot of athletes in those classes, but it overflowed with high-achieving, academically minded students commonly referred to as nerds. I had always considered myself way too cool, popular, and polished to be branded a nerd, but there I was in "their" world, which was just as much mine. And I made lifelong friends there, just as I had on the football field and basketball court.

I had a lifetime of experience being the minority in spaces viewed as reserved for the majority. I became adept at adapting to my surroundings and being comfortable being myself no matter where I was or whom I was around. This skill, this being able to be at home "from the streets to the suites," has been the story of my life. Each step of the way, from grade school to college to law school to the state senate, the mayor's office, and then the CEO seat with the National Urban League, I have lived experiences mastering the ditch, mastering the ability to operate, influence, and lead effectively no matter my surroundings. Whether it's discussing global economic policies with international heads of state or chopping it up with the fellas in a Ninth Ward barbershop, my ditch experiences have allowed me to be me and feel comfortable—wherever.

SECTION THREE OF *THE GUMBO COALITION* HIGHLIGHTS TWO KEY LEADERSHIP LESSONS:

- "Ants versus Crabs"—A Leader Knows When to Lead and When to Follow
- "Working the Room"—A Leader Builds Networks with Intention

So many of the victories in my life have come thanks to this ability to build coalitions between and among varying constituencies and demographics. So many of the successes in my life have come thanks to this ability to work the room, meet people of all stripes, form relationships, and lay the groundwork for potential collaborations. Chapters seven and eight delve into these critical skills.

CHAPTER 7

ANTS VERSUS CRABS

A LEADER KNOWS WHEN TO LEAD AND WHEN TO FOLLOW

The biting cold of February 2010 in Washington, DC, was the exact opposite of the warm reception we received in the Oval Office. As the Urban League president, I was among the leaders of the nation's most revered civil rights organizations. We were greeted by President Barack Obama, and his welcome set the tone for the day.

Our heart-to-heart that day allowed for straight talk and respectful disagreements while also revealing ample common ground. There was a sense of unity that underscored our very reason for the gathering. Preaching truth to power, often hard truths, had been standard operating procedure for leaders of the civil rights community. However, there was nothing standard about operating during the administration of the nation's first African American president. With the election of President Obama, conversations began within the civil rights community on how best to proceed.

One side pressed that, as the long-standing moral conscience of the country, our challenging and holding presidents accountable was task number one. Others, however, countered that criticizing President Obama would be to ignore the context of his presidency and miss the astoundingly unique opportunity his election presented.

The NAACP's Ben Jealous, the National Council of Negro Women's Dorothy Height, the National Action Network's Rev. Al Sharpton, and me, representing the National Urban League, were invited to that February meeting. All of us except the esteemed Dorothy Height attended. Dr. Height, being ninety years old, simply could not chance overexposure to the dangerous cold.

Another integral player to our efforts who also did not attend the meeting was Melanie Campbell. Campbell, longtime president of the National Coalition for Black Civic Participation, had been a friend of mine for many years and had recently started the Black Women's Roundtable to sharpen her advocacy around women. She had been a staffer for the late Maynard Jackson, mayor of Atlanta. Campbell, an alumna of Clark Atlanta University, brought down-to-earth, no-nonsense advocacy to our conversations.

Jealous was the relatively new president of the NAACP. When elected at age thirty-five, he became the organization's youngest national leader. Jealous was a Californian who went to Columbia and was a Rhodes Scholar. A passionate organizer, he was an activist and coalition builder.

Sharpton, best known for his work in New York, began his career as a protégé of Rev. Jesse Jackson in Operation Breadbasket out of the Southern Christian Leadership Conference. A gifted orator and preacher, Sharpton exhibited a level of political savvy and insight that belied how some contractors viewed him. When I moved to New York to become president of the National Urban League, it was Sharpton who embraced me with open arms.

What I brought to the meetings with President Obama was experience being in multiple Oval Office meetings before his presidency. I had been in regular White House meetings with George W. Bush and in regular Oval Office meetings with Bill Clinton. I often attended because of my positions as mayor of New Orleans, president of the National Urban League, and head of the United States Conference of Mayors. My role was for us, those in the room meeting with the commander in chief, to be clear and assertive about what we planned to talk about, because you never have enough time when you meet with the president of the United States. It was also my role to make sure we were clear about our takeaways.

In our meeting, the discussion with the president and his advisors was wide-ranging, covering everything from the recovery plan and its impact on Black America to judicial appointments and health care. We pressed the president on the need for the recovery plan to do more to benefit Black America where the unemployment rate had spiked to nearly 20 percent. We walked out believing that we had made important points and had established a dialogue with the new president and his team. This group of leaders proceeded with our meeting, only to discover afterwards that two nationally known and deeply respected figures, my friends Tavis Smiley and Dr. Cornel West, had labeled us as sellouts. They claimed we offered President Obama nothing of substance for the creation of a black agenda for his administration—that our meeting with number forty-four was just a shuck-and-jive tap dance bowing in subservience to the commander in chief.

For those who don't know, Smiley and West before their harsh stances against President Obama were household names in the black community, respected and revered for their social commentary, political stances, and advocacy for the underserved and under-represented.

To classify Smiley as a talk show host does not do justice to the breadth and depth of his reach within the hearts and minds of black Americans. Smiley hosted *BET Talk*, later named *BET Tonight*, a public affairs discussion show. He hosted *The Tavis Smiley Show* from 2002–04 on National Public Radio and served as host of a show simply named *Tavis Smiley* on the Public Broadcasting Service and *The Tavis Smiley Show* on Public Radio International.

Before this, Smiley had been a frequent and highly popular commentator on the *Tom Joyner Morning Show*, a nationally syndicated radio show broadcast on black and urban stations in the United States. Smiley and Joyner frequently supported each other's social action advocacy efforts. Smiley had already come to be a trusted voice within the black community before his stint with Joyner's show, but that experience catapulted him to the level of respected and revered thought leader. In fact, when Smiley was fired from BET in 2001, it was Joyner along with a sizeable portion of his radio audience that rallied, though unsuccessfully, to Smiley's defense.

One year before the BET firing, Smiley began hosting annual The State of the Black Union national town hall meetings, which were aired live on C-SPAN. These meetings focused on a specific topic affecting the African American community and featured a who's who panel of African American leaders, educators, and professionals to discuss and offer solutions to the forum's topic. Smiley also began building a national reputation as a political commentator, with countless appearances on MSNBC's, ABC's, and CNN's political discussion shows.

Cornel West, son of a Baptist minister, is a prominent and provocative democratic intellectual. He has also been called an American philosopher, political activist, social critic, author, and public intellectual. West focuses primarily on the role of race, gender, and class in American society. He is professor of the practice of public philosophy at Harvard University and holds the title of professor emeritus at Princeton University. He has also taught at Union Theological Seminary, Yale, Harvard, and the University of Paris. West graduated magna cum laude from Harvard in three years and obtained his MA and PhD in philosophy at Princeton.

Additionally, West has written twenty books and has edited thirteen others. The literary work considered his classic is *Race Matters*. But West has reached hearts, minds, and audiences in other ways as well. West is a frequent guest on *Real Time with Bill Maher*, CNN, C-Span, and *Democracy Now*.

He has also appeared in more than twenty-five films, including *The Matrix Reloaded* and documentaries like *Examine Life*, *Call + Response*, *Sidewalk*, and *Stand*. He has produced three spoken-word albums, collaborating with Prince, Jill Scott, André 3000, Talib Kweli, KRS-One, and the late Gerald Levert. Always the communicator, West's spoken-word interludes are featured on productions by Terence Blanchard, Raheem DeVaughn, Bootsy Collins, and more.

Even more so than Smiley, West was, and for some still is, considered a monumental force as a thought leader in the African American community. Any national gathering of black people discussing the issues, challenges, solutions, and opportunities before black people and others was considered lacking by many if Cornel West was not a principal player.

It is not hyperbole to say that if there had been a contemporary African American Mount Rushmore built prior to 2008, or more specifically, prior to the election of Barack Obama, one or both of them, West and Smiley, would see their busts memorialized.

Amazingly, though Smiley and West worked together to host their own radio talk show, *Smiley & West*, from 2010 to 2013, from my perspective most African Americans had absolutely no clue then and are probably learning about their joint venture for the first time at this reading. How is it possible that two individuals so respected, so revered, so beloved, and so active in their public appearances have done a show together that their own fan base has little to no clue even existed? I contend, it is because they didn't know when to lead and when to follow.

West and Smiley had already chosen their path. They were going to confront and call out the president whenever and wherever possible, to hold him accountable to the West-Smiley black agenda. What their efforts devolved into was something that felt way less noble than their original aim.

My group, on the other hand, chose a different route. We would still honor our charge to preach truth to power, but we believed the best way to do so in this unprecedented situation was by taking what I call the "ant route."

I have been a spiritual person my entire life. As such, I have probably heard somewhere around 12.7 million sermons in my lifetime. On way more than one occasion I have heard priests, rabbis, imams, preachers, and pastors allude to analogies from the natural world to make their spiritual, divine points. A common topic of these theologians has been ants.

Ants are miracles of nature for many reasons, and they are favorites of preachers offering sermonic directions on coalition building, cooperation, teamwork, community, and group responsibility. Simply put, the way ants consistently and doggedly work together make them nature's poster child for individuals doing their tasks, working in harmony with their collective.

Ministers, especially those out of the black preaching tradition, often spotlight another animal from the natural world in their weekly addresses—crabs. In the black community, this sermon is preached not only in churches by ordained clergy but anywhere black people congregate with anyone trying to make a point. We speak of the crabs-in-a-barrel syndrome—the crab practice of pulling fellow crabs down as one attempts to rise up from a bottom-of-the-barrel existence.

The lesson—don't be a crab; don't hate your sister's or brother's attempts at advancement so much that you actively work to pull them down. Rather, be an ant. Work in harmony with others so that you reflect the wisdom of the ancient African proverb that states, "When spider webs unite they can tie up a lion." The meaning? We can do more together than we can apart.

The conversation civil rights organization leaders had among ourselves was, in essence, a discussion about the path we would take in dealing with this new president. Would we be crabs or ants? We chose the ant route.

Tavis Smiley and Cornel West, both friends of mine, chose to hold the president accountable with the same zeal they applied to past presidents. However, many in the black community, including me, viewed their actions as applying a level of zeal the two had never shown before, even beginning their critiques of President Obama and his work before the ink dried on his inauguration programs.

As an aside, I will never forget that meeting. In my position with the National Urban League, I had been privy to attending several meetings in the Oval Office in the past. As I sat down that day and casually looked around the room, however, I noticed that everybody in the room was black, from the president to the three of us and the three staff persons accompanying him, who included Valerie Jarrett.

Jarrett is an amazing person in her own right. With a bachelor's degree from Stanford University and a Doctorate of Jurisprudence from the University of Michigan Law School, Jarrett worked in corporate and real estate law until 1987. She then moved into politics when she became deputy counselor for finance and development in the administration of Chicago's iconic, game-changing mayor, Harold Washington. After Washington's death, Jarrett remained with the mayor's office and accepted several positions in the administration of his successor, Richard M. Daley, including a stint as Daley's deputy chief of staff and later as a planning commissioner.

Jarrett was also chair of the Chicago Transit Authority from 1995 to 2003, and she served as chairman of the board for the Chicago Stock Exchange from 2004 to 2007. Before that, Jarrett was the executive vice president of the Habitat Company, a property management firm responsible for overseeing portions of Chicago's public housing system. In 2007, Jarrett became CEO of the Habitat Company.

What I have shared about Jarrett would be enough to rank her as a respected and diverse professional. But this look into Jarrett's resume does not even begin to speak to why she is most known and most revered.

Jarrett was associated with Barack Obama and his wife, Michelle, long before they became the president and First Lady. Jarrett hired then Michelle Robinson (before she had married Barack Obama) as an assistant in 1991 while working for Daley. Jarrett developed an ongoing personal and professional relationship with the couple and served as the finance chair of Obama's 2004 Senate campaign and was treasurer of his political action committee.

During Obama's presidential campaign, Jarrett mediated between Obama and members of the African American community who were concerned about the implications of his candidacy, especially since nearly the entire membership of the Congressional Black Caucus were initially Hillary Clinton supporters. Thus, Jarrett was also the obvious choice to serve as an envoy to those who had supported Clinton, Obama's primary rival for the Democratic nomination.

After Obama's election in November 2008, Jarrett served as cochair of his transition team and was then appointed senior advisor to Obama, a role she served in from 2009 to 2017.

Jarrett became a highly influential member of Obama's inner circle and a forceful advocate of his agenda. Jarrett helped Obama win reelection in 2012, and, as mentioned, she continued to serve as senior advisor until his second term ended in 2017. Most recently, Jarrett wrote the memoir *Finding My Voice: My Journey to the West Wing and the Path Forward* (2019). While Obama was still in office Jarrett was our go-to person on all civil rights issues, assisted over the years by Michael Blake, Heather Foster, Stephanie Young, Monique Dorsainvil, and Yohanes Abraham.

In fact, Jarrett was essential for setting up our February 2010 meeting with the president, a discussion that was frank. Specifically, we urged Obama to target his economic stimulus program on the high-poverty, high-unemployment areas of the nation, many of the black communities where the official unemployment rates raged at 16 percent, levels that had not been seen since the Great Depression.

That meeting, however, and its aftermath of Smiley-West comments, proved quite revealing. It revealed that Smiley and West had firmly made their decision, as we had made ours. Sharpton, Jealous, and I, along with others not in the meeting, decided not to be crabs but to be constructive with this unique opportunity. We chose to take the route of the ants.

We believed if we could build relationships with President Obama, we could influence him personally. I firmly believe that our decision paved the way for the opportunities we had to impact much of what Obama did during his first term. Further, we established the groundwork for his second four years.

Still, it should be understood that the National Urban League has always attempted to engage with every president at the outset of his term. So very often in the past, however, the lion's share of their policies and positions dictated, to varying degrees, that we play our traditional prophetic role of speaking hard truths to those in power—complete with biting criticisms and condemnations where necessary. I believed President Obama deserved that same initial opportunity, that same invitation to an open door of engagement.

Neither Smiley nor West afforded him that opportunity. And I dare say, had any of the past presidents we met with championed polices we believed were in the best interest of all of "We the People," our dealings would have been much more in tune with our dealings with President Obama.

What my friends West and Smiley got terribly wrong about our February 2010 Oval Office meeting was that our hope for open engagement with Obama did not mean we took the path of being a rubber stamp for anything he said or did. We didn't take the position that we would never disagree with him. In fact, we could have easily been on the front page of every paper in the country had we taken that route. I can't tell you how many calls I received from network TV, print media, and cable news reporters asking leading questions, fishing for harsh and critical words from me blasting the president for this or that. Had ego been my motivating factor, or that of the others in our fraternal order, we would have been so busy on the round of talks shows, we wouldn't have gotten anything else done.

Our meeting with President Obama and the invitation for positive engagement didn't mean we swore oaths of fealty and blind obedience. It meant critiques would come in the form of private conversations rather than via social media callouts or purposefully provocative interview quotes.

And believe me, there was nothing the press wanted more than to quote members of the civil rights community critiquing, criticizing, and condemning our nation's forty-fourth president. Daily I received calls from reporters goading, baiting, and pushing me to criticize President Obama. The bigger story would have been Obama working with national black leaders and organizations, but the press was wholly uninterested in that.

That's not what the press wanted. After the eruption in Ferguson, Missouri, over the shooting death of Michael Brown, members of the press called, asking, "Should the White House be doing more?" After the senseless killing of Trayvon Martin by George Zimmerman, the self-appointed judge, jury, and executioner of a seventeen-year-old child guilty of nothing but walking home from a local convenience store, the press called, asking, "Should the White House be doing more?"

After the deaths of Sandra Bland, Eric Garner, Freddie Gray, Philando Castile, and others, the press called, asking, "Should the White House be doing more?" They wanted a family feud in the black community in the worst way, but we vowed not to give it to them. We vowed not to succumb to the crabs-in-a-barrel mentality. We would push the Obama administration through direct conversations with Valerie Jarrett, Eric Holder, and the president himself.

It was clear that grassroots, street-level activism, including the emerging Black Lives Matter, were creating a strong social movement in favor of change.

Our position was about real strength. It was not about subservience but rather real leadership. Fake, wannabe leaders are obsessed with being in charge of everything and everyone, everywhere, every time. But grounded, confident, effective leaders have the ability to read situations as a great speaker can read a room. Real leaders recognize the powerful leadership value of knowing when to lead and when to follow.

Additionally, I don't think that some of our critics really felt the pulse of their constituents—the people for whom they said they took their aggressively antagonistic stance toward their dealings with President Obama.

In my estimation, they made a critical miscalculation. Their constituents were screaming for people in high places to support the first black president and bristled at what they saw as unwarranted attacks. When the negative attacks came, the chorus heard 'round the world was, "There they go, crabs in a barrel."

Now, to their defense, real leaders are willing to step out and offer their constituents what they believe those individuals need, even if it is neither popular nor what the people asked for. This position, which every leader will have to take at some point (or many points) during their tenure, comes from the notion that the leader knows best and that the followers will at some later point recognize the efficacy of the leader's decision. But there are just as many, if not more, moments when leaders need to submit to the will and whims of the people under their charge. It goes back to that critical leadership quality of knowing when to lead and when to follow. Because the leader who gets too far out in front of his students, employees, or constituents may look back and find that nobody's following.

Bottom line, leaders, you have to know your constituency, their wants, needs, expectations, hurts, fears, and challenges. Whether serving as a school leader, with faculty and students as your constituents, or as the head of a nonprofit with volunteers, community members, and board members as those to whom you answer, its critical to know where they stand on issues of importance—even on issues of tone used to conduct your business.

Some people mistake the person out front as the leader. Others believe the leader is the one they think looks the part. Others mistake the loudest, most talkative person in the room for the leader, the one with the most confidence and the most to say. Sometimes this is true. But I challenge you to watch real leaders working a room. Sure they're engaging, and they speak with as many people as is effective for their agenda. But many times, these leaders are not the ones raising the volume of the room, talking loud and saying nothing.

More often than not, in a conversation they're mainly listening—and learning. And when they speak, their words are directed and purposeful, rather than meant to impress or regale. Real leaders don't have to be the one speaking all the time. Real leaders don't have to be the ones leading all the time either.

I know this in a very personal and intimate way because I'm married—with teenage children still at the house. So even though I may be captain of the National Urban League ship, when I come home, nobody cares what I say or what I want to do. Whether it's what's for dinner, where are we going tonight, what work needs to be done around the house, who's coming over, my family may be loving, but they're not even trying to hear me. And I've learned that choosing to follow in that situation has made for a pleasant family dynamic. Although if you ask them, they'll say I'm in charge all the time.

More seriously, I have chaired and served on multiple national public and private sector boards throughout my career. On one, I carved out my role as the facilitator—designating ahead of time who will present what parts of the agenda, often recapping takeaways. As someone who likes to be in charge, I find I sometimes have to mute myself in meetings I'm not chairing. And that's okay. I'm not being fake or untrue to myself when I do that. I'm recognizing that neither I nor anyone else can lead every room you walk into.

Leaders recognize those rooms, those situations, where it does them more good to take a secondary role than to be out front. The ability to know when to lead and when to follow is priceless, especially when it comes to coalition building. Other leaders recognize your confidence and your respect for their leadership. Knowing when to lead and when to follow not only builds character, it builds relationships and coalitions.

TIGER TEAMS

Tiger Teams, I believe, sharpen this skill for all involved. Tiger Teams are a good example of using the tenets of when to lead and when to follow. What are Tiger Teams? Most people call them work groups, but I like the military terminology better here. And though the military uses the term to describe teams going on the attack, usually for destructive purposes, I like the idea of a group working together to "attack" a problem or challenge to come up with a solution for a very specific assignment.

For certain National Urban League projects, instead of assigning a task to a specific department, I create a Tiger Team designated to handle that business. The annual NUL conference, for example, is one of those assignments that works so much better when a Tiger Team takes the reins rather than this department or that.

The advantage of a Tiger Team is that they are interdisciplinary—meaning each department in our organization is represented. This means, the twenty to twenty-five folk assigned to the team come with perspectives related to their area. I am dead set against organizing in silos. It makes no sense to me to have one department organize an initiative and then hand it over to the marketing team and say, "Have at it; sell this to the world." It makes no sense to me to create a new initiative and then ask the money minds to figure out how we're going to fund it.

Tiger Teams allow for every area of the organization to have input, which then sharpens the final product because all things have been considered, from multiple angles. And each Tiger Team member is responsible for keeping their respective departments in the loop. This means the maximum number of people understand the big picture rather than only their role in it. It's like the person working on an auto assembly line. She may know how to affix the passenger side door to the chassis but be totally unaware of how her role fits into all the other assignments. To me, that gives employees too much room for disengagement. And that's not good. I have found that everyone is stronger, better, and more engaged when they know how their role fits into the bigger picture and how it relates to folk in other departments.

But the most powerful thing about Tiger Teams is the leadership dynamic.

Those sitting around the Tiger Team table are on equal footing. Everyone knows that, when they're on a Tiger Team, titles get thrown out the window. And often, the person in charge of a particular aspect of the Tiger Team's work won't be a manager or executive but rather one of those worker bees getting their chance to shine as a leader.

This gives others a chance to lead and allows those with the titles to master the art of following. I clearly designate the leaders of the Tiger Teams so that everyone understands their roles. This practice has improved engagement while increasing the level of respect for employees at all levels. These Tiger Teams have most definitely been a win-win for the National Urban League. And the secret sauce to their success has been that they enforce and reinforce the idea that a real leader recognizes when to lead and when to follow.

GUMBO COALITION RECAP: LEADERS KNOW HOW AND WHEN TO FOLLOW

Tiger Teams are akin to a working group that has a specific project, event, or objective that individuals from various departments within an organization work on for a defined period of time.

Tiger Team Setup

Tiger Team Setup—When a project or initiative requires a significant degree of collaboration and cooperation among departments, functions, and units.

Tiger Team Execution—Empower a chair or co-chair and a group of team members to carry out a project or initiative within a specific period of time.

Tiger Team Structure—A Tiger Team usually operates on a structure different than the one that usually exists within the organization. On a Tiger Team, an executive may report to a "subordinate," especially if the temporary assignment can best be met with that structure.

CHAPTER 8

WORKING THE ROOM

A LEADER BUILDS NETWORKS WITH INTENTION

My father, Ernest Nathan "Dutch" Morial, a native of New Orleans, graduated from Xavier University and became the first African American to earn a law degree from Louisiana State University. As a practicing attorney, my father made his name dismantling segregation on the battlefield of Louisiana courtrooms and as head of the local NAACP chapter. Before eventually becoming New Orleans' first black mayor in 1978, he had several unsuccessful bids for elected office. He did not give up. It was persistence that helped him become the first black member of the Louisiana State Legislature since Reconstruction (1967), the state's first black juvenile court judge (1970), and the first black elected to the Louisiana Fourth Circuit Court of Appeal (1974).

What many miss when telling the story of Dutch Morial is that he came from very humble, working-class beginnings. His father, my paternal grandfather, Walter Etienne Morial, was a cigar maker. He traced his roots back to a very proud and hardworking people in

Haiti. These were people whose level of dignity and regality would lead you to believe they were much higher on the socioeconomic scale than they were. They carried with them an air of confident assurance that belied their working-class reality.

My mother, Sybil Haydel Morial, also a native of New Orleans, was very down to earth, much like her husband. However, she and my father came from two different worlds. Unlike my father, my mother grew up middle class. Though she, too, began her higher education journey at Xavier, she went to graduate school at Boston University, where she befriended a classmate who went on to make a name for himself—Rev. Dr. Martin Luther King Jr.

One of my mother's closest childhood friends, Andrew Young, would also grow up to befriend King. Young also went on to serve as a US congressman representing Georgia, US Ambassador to the United Nations, and mayor of Atlanta.

Her father, my maternal grandfather, Clarence C.C. Haydel, graduated from Howard University before becoming a noted surgeon. Almost the entirety of my mother's people can trace their beginnings back to Louisiana's famous Whitney Plantation, which is now a museum devoted to slavery, a special place created by lawyer John Cummings, a man with a deep commitment to social justice. The Whitney Plantation and its two thousand acres was featured in Quentin Tarantino's movie *Django Unchained*.

From these beginnings eventually came my mother, a young lady socializing in circles beyond my father's reach. Yet, somehow, these people from those two different worlds met, married, and created not only a family and life but a legacy of service, advocacy, and civil rights. So it stands to reason that I seemed bred for that existence, for being comfortable operating in my own realities of two different worlds.

Throughout the ditch-crossing, dual-world experience my parents afforded me, not only was I learning how to feel comfortable in my skin in any situation, but I was internalizing the finer points of how to communicate. I was learning the critical importance of a word overused but not practiced enough by aspiring leaders—networking.

Leadership is multifaceted. It's not just communication, not just vision, not just execution, and not just that important combination of strength and compassion. Leadership is a fine mixture of all those, like a big band combines all instruments, sounds, and talents into one force, one sound. And nowhere is this melodic combination on display more openly and powerfully than where networking is on full display.

Networking is purposeful and intentional relationship building. Human interaction forms the basis of all business, politics, and most everything else. Networking is walking into a room with a plan and with the intention of leaving that room with an expanded personal universe of relationships. It's having a purpose in any and every social setting you find yourself in.

Networking is not about simply making friends in the traditional sense. As a leader, you certainly recognize the difference between your personal friends and your work friends. Work friends are more than associates; they are people with whom you form real bonds and relationships. But neither of you expects to spend holidays together or exchange birthday cards. You respect each other and, through learning about one another, come to like and understand each other, which more often than not makes working together more effective.

Networking is more listening to other people's words, dreams, and aspirations and allowing them to share rather than seeking to be the focal point of all conversations. It's showing interest in other people's stories. It's breaking through the walls of unfamiliarity and awkwardness and connecting with, learning about, and getting to know people on a social level. The astute leader realizes it's in these social settings, these networking opportunities, that captains of industry determine whom they can and can't work with.

THE TYPES OF NETWORKERS

There are many classifications of networkers. First you have the "super outgoing personalities." One of the greats in my circle is a childhood friend, Winston Burns. His ability to befriend and remember the connection between people, places, and things is an art and God-given talent.

Burns, a graduate of the esteemed Morehouse College, became a banker before working in the music industry. Afterwards, he became an entrepreneur. He and his wife have become wildly successful in their business undertakings. To say Burns knows a lot of people is a gross understatement to the power of his networking powers. He is the kind of person for which the saying "has never met a stranger" was created.

Next you have the "Rolodexers." These are the people with a list of contacts that can get them one degree away from anyone they could possibly want to meet. For example, take Jimmy Fitzmorris. He served as a New Orleans city council member and lieutenant governor of the state of Louisiana. Fitzmorris advised me early in my political career, offering insights and tidbits on local government. He had a penchant for sending personal, handwritten notes to those he met along his life's journey.

I don't know if I have ever met a soul who knew so many people. Just as impressive, Fitzmorris was never shy about connecting two people in his network. He was a walking encyclopedia and a veritable expert on who's who in New Orleans.

I observed him and parroted his attention to following up with people by collecting their business cards and following up with letters and phone calls. Over the years, I would receive news articles from him, articles about me including quotes I made. Additionally, he sent me articles about others in our circles and various articles on topics he thought I would be interested in. Fitzmorris built a legion of admirers and friends all around New Orleans.

Then there are the networkers I call the "advisors." The perfect example is Don Hubbard. Hubbard was a Congress of Racial Equality activist in the 1960s and founder and chairman of one of New Orleans' most influential political organizations, the Southern Organization for Unified Leadership.

His networking style was to serve as the wise man and confidential advisor to legions of political leaders. Never one interested in running for public office, he has been a quintessential king maker, quietly guiding the careers and moves of others. A chess master when it comes to politics, Hubbard also possesses the uncanny knack of connecting people, mediating disputes, and never leaving any footprints.

Finally, we have my mother, Sybil Morial, a classic example of the "civic activist" networker. By serving as an active volunteer on numerous civic, community, education, and private boards, she built up an incredible Rolodex of people from all walks of life in New Orleans. When she and her friends, mostly African American teachers, were denied membership in the League of Women Voters in the early 1960s because they were black, they started their own civic education and voter registration organization, the Louisiana League of Good Government, which amassed thousands of members in less than a decade. My mother's networking style stands for paying dues in an unselfish way and thereby creating goodwill, leverage, and credits with the people with whom you serve.

She undoubtedly learned her approach from her father, Dr. C. C. Haydel, grandson of a slave, 1922 graduate of Howard University's School of Medicine, and principal shareholder of Standard Life Insurance Company. Her father and my grandfather were active in numerous fraternal, civic, and religious organizations and my grandfather served as a board member of the Urban League of Greater New Orleans in the 1950s. He joined with other African American professionals to organize a fundraising event for Rev. Dr. Martin Luther King Jr. in 1957 when he came to the city to a meeting of the Southern Christian Leadership Conference.

Networking is about working the room. This by no means implies nefarious intent, but it does demand intent. And it demands other qualities I had honed thanks to my life experiences. However, for those who don't have life experiences and exposures similar to mine, there are a myriad of things you can do to become a formidable networker.

First, it helps immensely if you are innately curious, a self-learner and nonjudgmental. Recognizing there's a world beyond yours and being curious and open-minded about the ideas, viewpoints, and aspirations of these other dimensions helps. You would be surprised how many people have almost zero awareness of ideas and opinions outside their own mental "compound."

Being aware of ideas and opinions other than your own is a critical starting point. Appreciating how divergent viewpoints may help you look at your own beliefs in new ways is a powerful tool for opening yourself to new networks. These new ways of looking and seeing and understanding things also allow you to view challenges and opportunities differently. These new perspectives allow you to become even more curious about what others have to say. You become more interesting to others because you become more interested in others. If you can get people talking, especially about themselves and something important to them, you're on the road to making an honest connection with another human being—a possible future employer, employee, or collaborator.

For the more introverted among us, starting conversations with strangers can seem daunting, if not impossible. What I've found most effective, coupled of course with my intent to make any social setting a networking opportunity, is to introduce, then ask. Introduce yourself, and then ask a question. A simple "How was your day?" or "How did you deal with the crazy traffic getting here?" gets people talking and, most importantly, talking about themselves.

Once the conversation has begun, listen. Even basic questions can hint at things important to them. Then ask about those things. When they respond, "My commute getting here was challenging because I first had to drop off my daughter at dance practice," the active listener hears family, and all things associated with that, as well as the presence of extracurricular activities in that person's life.

Because my two youngest children are in middle school and high school (soon to be college), respectively, and my oldest is a successful professional and college graduate, I have an instant connection. Also, because school is such a central factor in the Morial household, and because I'm naturally curious, I always want to know where people's children go to school and what things they are into.

But even for the person with none of those relationships, if you're curious and genuine, a perfectly acceptable follow-up would sound something like, "Wow, being single and without children, I can't even imagine what that's like. How do you pull off family, career, and . . ." Once the ice is broken, real connections can take place.

If it's not a natural part of who you are, one way to boost your curiosity is to travel the world. And if globetrotting is out of your price range, travel the world within your own community. Most major cities are havens for diverse cultures. Culture-specific food festivals, celebrations, gatherings, and so much more are weekly and daily happenings that offer opportunities for you to step out of your monochromatic existence. From there, you can connect with people who operate outside the parameters of your life and expand your understanding and comfort level with them. This is where the connections and relationships you've made come in handy. They can serve as your guide or entranceway to these new settings and opportunities.

I often ask C-level leadership, "When was the last time you actually visited your business?" This question sounds silly and nonsensical to entrepreneurs, but a large number of top-level executives of *Fortune 500* companies only know their companies from a boardroom or spreadsheet perspective. I challenge these individuals to invest time in making that trip. Speaking to living, breathing souls on the ground can not only provide insights that a spreadsheet cannot, it expands the length and breadth of your relationships. It also helps build your confidence in being able to speak and connect with those with whom you hold little in common.

I also challenge leaders to go to lunch with people who don't look like them or think like them. This is a simple, easy way to break ourselves out of the natural ruts and corners we often push ourselves into. I also suggest that bosses and parents share their worlds and other worlds with their employees and children as often as possible. The key is to make it a habit to cross those invisible ditches in your own life that segregate you from others. Being able to feel at home in any setting while meeting new people is priceless.

It's amazing what unexpected, unplanned, and unscripted moments arise from simply stepping out into those networking waters. The Gumbo Coalition became the official and unofficial slogan of both my mayoral campaign and my entire life—actively mixing different ingredients into one powerfully delicious dish. The members of my mayoral cabinet were referred to by others and often by themselves as the Gumbo Coalition. Any citywide initiatives that demanded coalitions and collaborations between various parties were deemed members of the Gumbo Coalition.

The movement to bring professional basketball to New Orleans was viewed as the work of the Gumbo Coalition. In truth, it was a testament to regional networking across political, geographic, and ideological lines in southeastern Louisiana.

The Gumbo Coalition's promotion and appeal helped in large part convince the National Basketball Association that the city of New Orleans was safe, welcoming, and hungry enough to support an NBA franchise.

It's thanks to the Gumbo Coalition that we could talk the National Football League out of changing the location of Super Bowl XXXVI in 2002. Because of 9/11, the original date of the Super Bowl was pushed back a week to February 3, 2002. But the Superdome was already booked for that day. The NFL decided a change of venue might be the only viable solution since our city was locked into the other event's contract. Behind the scenes, I communicated with the entity that had a signed contract for February 3, the local leaders of our hospitality industry, and NFL officials to convince them that under no circumstances would New Orleans relinquish the Super Bowl.

What I did behind closed doors we duplicated during our city's efforts to attract the NBA to our fair city. This time, however, while I worked behind the scenes with a team of people, our efforts were greatly enhanced by the very public, active, and vocal efforts of the good people of New Orleans who came together to show the NBA that the NBA belonged in New Orleans. There were posters and signage and T-shirts emblazoned with the words everywhere.

Had social media existed when I ran for mayor, I'm certain the Gumbo Coalition would have gone viral, because it is still so much a part of the conversation about the recent history of New Orleans.

In my initial campaign for mayor, I urged my team to get in front of people, to get in rooms with people to simply meet them. Sure, our campaign needed donations as any campaign does. But my emphasis was not mainly focused on money. Rather, I wanted to meet individuals, couples, and families and for them to meet and get to know me. I believed that I was my strongest selling point. I had confidence that, if people ever had a chance to meet me, they would be way more inclined to hear what I had to say and seriously consider my vision as a plan for the city they could get behind.

We organized what had to be hundreds of house parties. We had parties in St. Charles Avenue mansions, as well as in public housing apartments, beauty salons, and neighborhood bars. The concept wasn't original. Most politicians who used it, however, focused on securing donations and monetary pledges. I simply wanted a chance to meet people, to connect with people. It was the quintessential working-the-room lab.

During one such event, the host happened to be cooking gumbo. It hit me that instant that what I sought to do with New Orleans is what the city's many great chefs in households rich and poor did in their kitchens regularly—fix gumbo. So during that house party, off the top of my head I started talking about how a good gumbo has to start with roux, a combination of a brown base and white flour, and how different vegetables and seafood were thrown in the pot together—different ingredients all with their own unique flavors coming together, working together to make something special, something delicious, something great, something quintessentially New Orleans. A member of the press happened to be in the room and coined the phrase *gumbo coalition* in his article. And it stuck. But it never would have emerged had it not been for those opportunities to connect with others, expand my relationships, and work the room.

Good leaders need to create networking opportunities for their teams so they can form relationships beneficial for intercompany communication and create a cohesive workplace. Any city or company initiative needs all departments moving in the same direction. Everyone has to be invested. And in our status meeting, this investment fueled a level of interdepartmental Q&A and collaboration that was magic. The people from marketing would ask questions that the finance office would have never been able to think of. Legal would come after both and offer their insights, which had to be considered.

Though these meetings weren't networking opportunities in the traditional sense, they did allow people who rarely saw, or even knew, each other to connect and work together, strategize, question, and come up with solutions—together. And the principles of working the room still applied. Everyone entered the space with intention. Connections were made. People got to know one another in ways that made our forward movement and success that much more possible.

This is where Tiger Teams come in. Remember from the last chapter that these are temporary teams with one assignment that they work on for a set period of time before disbanding. That means NUL members know at any time they could be called to join a team of individuals they barely know but who were assembled for a specific purpose—one important enough to pull them for weeks or months at a time from their regular work assignments. Success depends upon these individuals coalescing as a legitimate team, a united force.

Additionally, when I have big initiatives, I make certain that members of all departments attend our weekly status meetings. So often, organizations have departments that operate in isolation, in silos. The one, two, three, or six people who work in a given silo too often have little interaction with members of other silos.

I've known how important networking is since my twenties, when I began collecting business cards. I was fanatical about it. Still am. I would keep shoeboxes full of cards. And when Rolodexes hit the scene, I used those as well. Then as now, I did my best to follow up with my new contact with a note. Getting the business card allowed for one level of connection. The follow-up made the connection even stronger. I operated under the assumption that networking and being able to work the room mattered because who you know does actually make a difference. Moreover, I could never know if who I met in any given setting could one day become a close friend, a business partner, or someone I could call on for help or advice, or vice versa. Hence, every connection, every interaction, was important and valued.

Not everyone is built for nonstop social engagement. Some folk have a knack and personality to meet people. Others don't and need help in the process. And that's okay. I've often seen those who consider themselves introverted muster up the energy and will to work the room when the time came to do so. They simply viewed their investment in social settings as a business task or challenge, and with that mind-set they were able to meet the challenge regularly. I've seen some less-social individuals team with someone, a work friend or a neighbor, to work the room in tandem.

Still, there are other ways to grow your network and improve your ability to communicate with people from multiple worlds. For some, joining and participating in organizations has been the most effective way to expand their relationships and contacts. These associations are often opportunities for people to learn other people's characters and get to know them on a less stressful level. Joining civic associations, faith communities, and alumni associations are ways people who are new to a city or neighborhood find like-minded people with whom to connect.

With millennials and members of Generation Z, social media has replaced their use of and appreciation for old-school methods of networking—that is, face-to-face encounters. And social media brings with it its own set of pros and cons. One huge pro is that you can connect with hundreds or thousands of people unrestrained by geography by simply logging on and engaging. It's one of the most powerful networking platforms ever created.

Countless global protests against injustice were organized through social media. The uprisings in Egypt in protest against antidemocratic forces was a social media phenomenon, as have been so many of the Black Lives Matter and #MeToo protests nationally since 2013. Social media has made hyper-networking possible in ways unimaginable just a few years ago.

The big drawback, however, is that so many people have come to depend on social media to replace the most powerful of all networking platforms—face-to-face interaction. I contend that social media doesn't replace face-to-face contact but rather enhances it. Just as eating out hasn't replaced eating at home, just as airplanes didn't make travel by train and car irrelevant, social media hasn't heralded the death of personal interactions. At least it shouldn't.

The most powerful way to network in the twenty-first century is to marry the two, the old school and the new, in ways that work best for you. And instead of seeing them as competitors, view them as complements. Leaders build organizations. And in so doing, leaders are called upon to use the best tools available. Social media and face-to-face interaction are two tools that can help build your personal network of contacts and help your employees and students do the same.

And just like gumbo, you can always add to it. During my initial campaign for mayor, my brother, Jacques Morial, saw that nobody focused on the Latino and Vietnamese communities. These two emerging communities were growing in numbers and, therefore, in electoral influence. The voter rolls did not identify them but simply classified them as "other." We knew better and created literature in Vietnamese and Spanish to let them know that we were interested in hearing their stories and inviting them to join our campaign. We reached out and built relationships with the leaders of those communities and committed meaningful roles in our administration. We were interested in sitting down and hearing their leaders' concerns. We were interested in making connections and forming relationships. We were making gumbo, and together we made history thanks to the power of communicating in multiple worlds—through the power of networking.

GUMBO COALITION RECAP: BUILDING NETWORKS WITH INTENTION

It's great to know people, but a transformative leader understands that people make the world go 'round. A leader recognizes that having a network is a necessity, not a convenience.

Building a Network

Demonstrate a Genuine Interest and Curiosity about Other People— Some people always talk about themselves and show no interest in others. Talent is God-given, fame is man-given, and conceit is self-given. I don't start conversations with people I meet for the first time talking about myself.

First Impressions Count—Keep it real. Practice your small talk. If you are not good at meeting people, get a wingman (or woman), someone who can help facilitate your introductions in social or business settings.

Recognize That There Are Different Kinds of Networks.

True-Blue—Close friends. Tend to be a smaller network.

Professional or Business Associates—They are people with whom you've had business dealings and/or projects over the years. There's a basis of trust between you.

Casual Friends—People in your circle that may be coemployees, church members, people you've been in professional clubs with, or classmates. You know them enough to say hello but have never had close dealings with.

Rent Your Rolodex—This is introducing friends to friends. I may call a friend and say, "I understand XYZ is a church member of yours. Do you know him well enough to introduce me to him?" That friend might ask me, "What do you want with him?" So be prepared to share your intentions so your friend will be comfortable enough to do the introduction. This is how you build credits. By renting your Rolodex, you open the door to your friend introducing you to someone you may need to know in the future.

Technology—A powerful networking tool to keep your relationships fresh is technology. Your ability to continue a conversation after you meet somebody was a method unheard of fifteen years ago. Friends can keep up with each other via LinkedIn, text, Facebook, and so on. Make sure you incorporate it in your networking plan.

SECTION FOUR

A KNOCK ON THE DOOR

Shortly after I passed the bar and became the first black lawyer at Barham & Churchill, I received a late-night knock at my door. It was members of the Shropshire family, a family I had known most of my life. I came to know the family when Lonnie Shropshire and I met and became close friends in high school. That I received a visit from his family, people I hadn't seen in at least seven years, would have normally been cause for celebration—even with the late hour of their surprise arrival. However, their reason for this nocturnal visit was far from pleasant in nature.

The family informed me that my friend Lonnie, their brother, had been arrested for burglary and wanted me to represent him. As a new lawyer at a downtown law firm that did not specialize in criminal law, I did not know if I could take this assignment for a man who was now in deep trouble, a man I had grown up with and befriended in high school. It was a long shot, but I informed the family that I would do everything in my power to convince those who ran the firm to give me the leeway to apply my skills in a case that was extremely personal.

Amazingly, I convinced the law firm to allow me to represent Lonnie pro bono. Not only did they agree, they provided me the assistance of a veteran lawyer by the name of Fredericka Homberg. Homberg, a former assistant United States attorney, now happens to be a well-respected Louisiana State Appellate Court judge.

With my firm fully supporting my desire to represent my friend, I took on the case. But early on in the process I faced the challenge of being unable to secure the police report that formed the basis of Lonnie's arrest. Common sense would suggest that if someone were accused of a crime and arrested, they and their legal representative would have access to the police report. However, I learned that criminal law in the great state of Louisiana did not give the accused access to these records.

Needless to say, I was outraged. In fact, I was absolutely livid that such an egregious omission of basic fairness had been allowed to exist as standard operating procedure in my home state. I shuddered to think about how many individuals accused and arrested for crimes had been convicted, sentenced, and incarcerated for an untold number of years even though there may have existed within those police reports information that may have led to different verdicts and far different life outcomes.

In my mind, just because it was the framework within which attorneys and criminal defendants had to maneuver for God only knows how long, this blocking of access was totally unacceptable. I began to look for a mechanism to get the records, since I thought they were essential to defending my client. To formulate a defense for Lonnie without seeing the police report would have been like being expected to take a final exam even though school policy forbade students from accessing critical textbooks. It made no sense to me. The whole situation wreaked of unfairness.

I looked for creative and innovative ways around what I viewed as merely a foolish loophole—even though it was state law. I say *loophole* because, in law, as in any other area of life, when faced with a challenge or roadblock, if you search long enough, you just may find a way around the obstruction. And that's exactly what I did. While engaged in my research, searching for that loophole, I came across the Louisiana Public Records Law, or Freedom of Information Act, which seemed to suggest that the police report I sought was part of the state's public documents—meaning, I should have easy access to them.

After being rebuffed by a veteran criminal court judge, Shirley Wimberly, I began a separate proceeding in civil district court to secure access to the records. I was able to convince a separate judge on the civil district court circuit, Judge Gerald Federoff, to rule in our favor and grant us access to the police report, which he did.

These conflicting rulings, the ruling from Wimberly denying me access and the ruling from Federoff granting it, ended up forming the basis of a case before the Louisiana Supreme Court. This case provided me with a rare opportunity as a newly minted lawyer to argue before the state's highest court in what was a major case in criminal discovery law.

As I prepared the case, Mack Barham, a founder of my law firm and a retired member of the Louisiana Supreme Court, said he would join me when I argued my case before the court. I was truly honored, because not only was Barham a distinguished former member of the state's supreme court, but he was known and revered as an expert on Louisiana law.

Recognizing the level of import this case carried, along with the incredible opportunity for me professionally to argue before the Louisiana Supreme Court, I never forgot that this case was as personal as a case could get. My friend's life and freedom were on the line. Thus I prepared probably harder than I had ever prepared anything in my life, which is really saying something. For I have never been afraid of hard work, or investing time far over and above what was required, to achieve goals that met the extremely high standards of conduct and accomplishment that my parents set for me and I had set for myself.

Needless to say, though, I was a very young, wet-behind-the-ears lawyer. I was supremely confident. I was ready to take on the world. Not only that, I had the incredible honor of walking side by side into the courthouse with one of its former members with statewide stature. It was go time. It was game time, and I was ready to take the field. What could possibly dim my light?

As Barham and I were about to enter the front door of the Louisiana Supreme Court, Barham stopped me on the steps and said, "You know, you're probably going to lose this case." I was a man stunned. I responded by not saying a word. But internally I was livid and somewhat offended.

Nonetheless, we went inside and I proceeded to argue before the court, giving it my very best. All of those hours, days, and weeks of preparation were paying off. Barham's words, instead of blinding me to my abilities, inspired me to let them show all the more. My argument was personal in large part because the case was personal, and not just because it involved my friend Lonnie.

I thought about all those other defendants throughout the years and over the course of decades, whose legal teams had been hamstrung by a simple legal omission. I was bringing my A game and I knew it. I could feel it. The feeling was similar to athletes who go off on the field or court and tell reporters after the game, "I was in the zone." That's exactly where I was—in the zone, giving it everything I had.

As we walked out of the building, Barham stopped me, sharing with me both a question and comment that have stayed with me over these many years. He asked me, "Where did you learn how to argue like that?" He then stated emphatically, "I have never seen an argument of that quality from a lawyer so young. And I must admit, I think you convinced the court to rule your way." I responded, "Sir, I've been a member of your law firm for a year now and feel like a star player who has been stuck on the bench. You need to put me in the game more often."

Needless to say, six weeks later, we got the ruling. The Louisiana State Supreme Court ruled 7–0 in our favor, making public records available to defendants for the first time in the state's history. Truly, persistence and innovation ruled the day. In this seminal case, I displayed persistence by not allowing myself to get flustered and frustrated by Judge Wimberley denying access to the critical police report. In addition, I showed innovation in securing an alternative route to get those denied records. I had crossed the proverbial ditch yet another time.

Two weeks after the court's decision, I decided to leave Barham & Churchill and begin my own law practice, a bold move that led to the beginning of a fulfilling and successful ten-year journey as a lawyer on my own.

Barham's words just before I entered the courtroom were hurtful. It was as if I were going into a basketball game to shoot free throws to clinch a victory and my head coach telling me, "You're probably going to miss those shots." Ouch. Who does that?

But I had to move beyond the pain. As I said, when I heard his words, I said nothing and remained focused. But inside of me, a deep, visceral fire burned in me igniting all the more my desire to win. Persistence allowed me to avoid succumbing to doubt or hurt or fear. Instead, I emerged feeling as if I had even more to prove.

Today, the Shropshire case is routinely cited in Louisiana criminal discovery requests. The case was won in large part due to the power of persistence. But it also owes a debt to innovation.

I innovated when I used a separate proceeding to get the records I needed to adequately defend my client. As I described, this innovation involved going the Freedom-of-Information route.

Many times, lawyers are taught to strictly follow procedures. This means lawyers don't always approach things creatively. That's a really polite way of saying most lawyers lack the nerve to color outside of the lines and do things differently to achieve their aims. Why was I so open to innovation? Because it was based more on research and instinct than anything else. Had I simply accepted the first ruling, we would not have gotten access to that report and the law would not have been changed.

Another reason why I was open to a creative, innovative way forward was because I revered those heroic civil rights lawyers who seemed to always make a way out of no way and tear the walls of segregation down brick by brick, legal case by legal case.

In this case, the reports had never been available. Through innovation and persistence, the law in Louisiana was changed, and criminal proceedings became a little bit fairer from that point on.

SECTION FOUR OF *THE GUMBO COALITION* HIGHLIGHTS TWO KEY LEADERSHIP LESSONS:

- "Persistence Is Always a Winning Formula"—A Leader Fights through Disappointments to Achieve Victory
- "Innovation Requires Seeing New Paths"—A Leader Must Seek New Ways to Solve Old Problems

In the following chapters I talk about persistence in the pursuit of an NBA franchise and innovation in the pursuit of corporate diversity and inclusion practices. Whether one is a lawyer, elected official, or business leader, persistence and innovation are always tools in one's arsenal to problem-solve and to advance an organization's agenda.

In the instance of innovation and corporate diversity, the MOU approach brought together the black, Latino, Asian, disabled, and LGBTQ community under one umbrella to fight for this corporate inclusion and diversity. While it was persistence that allowed us to stay that course until achieving success. Let's see how these two lessons can empower your leadership walk!

CHAPTER 9

PERSISTENCE IS ALWAYS A WINNING FORMULA

A LEADER FIGHTS THROUGH DISAPPOINTMENTS TO ACHIEVE VICTORY

When I became mayor of New Orleans, there were many challenges I wanted to tackle for the city's greater good: runaway crime, police department corruption run rampant, business divestment, and more. For the city I love, I wanted to enact a safety plan that made for safer streets and revived people's confidence in what the city could accomplish. For my hometown, I wanted to restore the community's trust in its police force by holding bad cops accountable and supporting and celebrating officers who brought honor to their calling. For the Big Easy, I wanted to be able to attract businesses and industry back to the city to add to the revenue brought in by our tourist industry.

These things were done for the people, for the city. But there was still something I wanted to accomplish for personal reasons. As a basketball super fan and former player from fourth grade through high school, I wanted to bring the NBA back to the Crescent City.

Sure, if I were successful, there would be numerous benefits to New Orleans' businesses and communities. Our city would prove we could attract and retain the largest scale businesses. Thousands of jobs would be generated for the city and surrounding areas. But bringing the NBA back to New Orleans was still very personal.

I vividly remembered as a boy often going to see the New Orleans Buccaneers, a charter member of the American Basketball Association. After the Buccaneers moved to another city in 1970, it would be nine years before New Orleans had another professional basketball team to cheer on. Still, from day one of the Jazz's stay in our city, I was right there with them, cheering them on. The pain the entire city felt was palpable when they, too, packed their bags and left us all in their rearview mirror, headed to Utah. Utah! Do they even know what jazz is?

As mayor of a major North American city, I had one heck of a platform from which to work, and I was determined to make something happen. But there were several hurdles to clear and multiple failed attempts to make before we struck gold. And believe me, without persistence, that success would have never found us.

I was under no illusions; I knew bringing the NBA back to New Orleans would be an uphill battle. The NBA commissioner during my tenure was David Stern, who in 1979 was the NBA's general counsel and remembered firsthand the dustup as the Jazz sought to leave town. And by dustup I mean my father, Mayor Dutch Morial, suing the NBA for leaving New Orleans and the bad blood that lingered between the city and the NBA as a result.

Our first shot at reclaiming NBA-city status came in the form of a group of businessmen from Minnesota who paid Governor Edwards and me a visit sharing their big plans to buy the Minnesota Timberwolves and move them to New Orleans. For our city's part, we were already engaged in building a new sports arena for basketball and hockey—even though we didn't have a basketball or hockey franchise in our city, hence no teams and no tenants. But our moxie impressed our guests from the Land of Ten Thousand Lakes.

This venture was derailed, however, when it became apparent that the Minnesota contingent comprised individuals who, in my opinion, were of questionable character. It turns out they misrepresented themselves and didn't have the financial wherewithal to buy the Timberwolves. Thus there would be no purchase of that franchise and move to our fair city.[1]

Afterwards, I visited David Stern in his office with Doug Thornton of the New Orleans Sports Foundation. Thornton was well connected and well respected both locally and nationally. He was a huge reason why New Orleans could bring the US Olympic Trials for track and field to the city in 1992. Thornton had that kind of juice and nerve and know-how. I felt good having him on our side as we tried to convince Stern, now NBA commissioner, to designate New Orleans as the next city to receive an NBA franchise. I felt even better about our chances when combining Thornton's track record with all of the great revitalization in the city: crime down, confidence in police up, businesses booming.

From my recollection, as we gathered in Stern's office, the first thing the commissioner said to me was, "I was around in the 1970s, and your father sued us." My response: "Yes, he was a fan of the litigation process." We had a good laugh, but I quickly surmised that Stern was slightly dismissive. I honestly think he couldn't fathom how New Orleans, a small-market city that had already lost an ABA and an NBA team, could possibly see itself as worthy and able to house an NBA team.

"You all don't even have a building or an owner," he said, stating the obvious. We informed him of the work we were doing to build an arena and that we wanted to be on the NBA's radar when a team became "available."

As Stern politely kicked us out of his office, he told us to go build a building and then come back and see him and that at the moment the NBA had no teams trying to move. Still reeling from failing to secure the Timberwolves, we now had strike two—the Stern brush-off—to add to our résumé.

We left that meeting and returned home, finishing our arena with no permanent tenants in 1999. Shortly thereafter, we learned that the Vancouver Grizzlies, one of two NBA teams in Canada, was struggling and up for sale. I also found out that the guy trying to buy the team was Michael Heisley, a former Georgetown classmate of Sam LeBlanc, chairman of the New Orleans Chamber and founding partner of one of New Orleans' largest law firms. LeBlanc was a former state legislator, candidate for mayor, and close supporter of mine. Like the Minnesota faction, Heisley was planning a purchase and a move. Unlike the Minnesota group, Heisley was well able to purchase the team and successfully did so. Now he needed only to decide on a destination between his three top choices: Memphis, Louisville, and New Orleans.

Louisville's plan included the parent company of KFC as one of its major partners. Its plan seemed solid and promising. So, too, did the Memphis plan to lure the Grizzlies. For our part, we thought we had the best option and the most to offer.

It just so happened, that in April 2001, I led a delegation to Israel of the US Conference of Mayors, a delegation that included Louisville's mayor, David Armstrong. One day while out visiting historic sites in the Holy Land, Armstrong's phone rang. It was Heisley. How did I know? I was standing right beside Armstrong, and I could hear the entire conversation. Heisley informed Armstrong that he was down to a short decision, and Louisville had a good, strong possibility of being the chosen city.

Thirty seconds later, my phone rang and Heisley told me the exact same thing. And because Armstrong was still standing by my side, he could hear this for himself. Man, we had a good laugh over that. We then wished each other good luck and played the usual game, each telling the other, "Looks like you got it. I hope you get the team," and so on. I don't know if Heisley ever found out that two of the three mayors waiting on his decision were halfway around the world, standing right next to each other. As I said, it was material for a good laugh.

But I was not in a laughing mood when I received word that the team ended up in Memphis. To say I was dejected and depressed would be an understatement. This was my last year in office due to term limits, and it appeared that my dream of bringing NBA basketball back to my hometown was going to remain just that—a dream. Strike three. And as any sports fan knows, three strikes and you're out. It certainly seemed that way.

A few months later, November to be exact, Doug Thornton called and said, "I think we have another option. Come over to my house so we can discuss." When I got there, he told me that the Charlotte Hornets had to leave their building because they lost a referendum to build a new arena. He added that the team's owner was a native of Mississippi, just across the border from New Orleans. In short, Thornton ran down several reasons why the Hornets had to get out of Charlotte.

My first response: "Are they playing us?" Thornton, a great judge of character and intentions, said he didn't think so. So even though we had already struck out, falling short three times, we decided then and there to go into game mode and take all meetings necessary and prepare all presentations possible to make our pitch for an NBA franchise.

Our first order of business was to meet with the Hornets' co-owner, Ray Woolridge, to find out if he was really serious about relocating his team. Woolridge told us straight up, "If you guys put the right package together, we're coming to New Orleans. Though I'm not the primary owner, I'm the one with the money and the one who will make the decision." He was serious.

So was the NBA, which set some very high benchmarks for us to get the league to approve the move; benchmarks that included a set number of pledges to purchase season tickets for a team not yet officially in the city and the city's commitment to build a new practice facility. We already had the arena. And we certainly had persistence. We were still in the game when logic would have suggested we give up and focus our energies and attention elsewhere. But we believed we just needed to get our Gumbo Coalition together to make magic happen.

Though Stern seemed skeptical about our chances and about New Orleans being a good fit for the NBA, he remained professional at all times in our many conversations while we ran our campaign to win the team, which included collecting the requisite pledges for season tickets. It included something else—a Gumbo Coalition with a large side of persistence.

Each of those past times when our attempts to lure an NBA team fell short, we took the time to learn a different valuable lesson that strengthened us. After the Vancouver Grizzlies situation, we realized the importance of mobilizing the entire community of residents, business leaders, and elected officials within the Greater New Orleans area. With that first Stern meeting, we saw the importance of having all our ducks in a row. After our Timberwolves loss, we knew that we had to prove New Orleans' fitness to Stern. We had to show every major business and political leader was on board to support the new team in specific, tangible ways. We had to demonstrate to the NBA's head honcho that we were unified and energetic enough to be a small-market success story, and that we showed this already by our success at reducing crime and bringing back a thriving economy.

This was the essence of persistence: learning from our past failures rather than wallowing in pity and not figuring out how to get stronger, better, more effective at making our case. With this Charlotte Hornets opportunity, we knew that our best chance at getting that team to make New Orleans its new home was to incorporate all those lessons while going public about our intentions and efforts in the biggest, loudest way possible. Quiet, clandestine efforts were not at all what was called for or needed if we wanted the NBA in New Orleans. We had to be loud and proud.

I cannot stress enough how appreciative I was of the Hornets' owner's candor when he essentially said, all BS aside, if you can put the package together, we're coming to New Orleans because you have a much more exciting city than any other options. His honesty helped because, as we were being painfully honest about our past efforts to lure a team, we also had to be honest about the other partners involved. In the Timberwolves situation, we were dealing with an entity of potential owners who lacked the integrity and financial power to come through. In our cold-call meeting with Stern, his reticence was a real factor. With the Vancouver Grizzlies, we were never given reliable, honest feedback on where we stood.

With this new opportunity with the Hornets, we knew where we stood. Moreover, the Charlotte opportunity differed from the Timberwolves one because it wasn't a sale and relocation. Rather, the Charlotte shot was simply owners looking to relocate. For us, that meant a much simpler process. Instead of two hurdles to clear (two separate issues the NBA would have to approve), we had just one.

Still, our plan wouldn't work without the power of a Gumbo Coalition.

We had to partner with state agencies to put together the right arena lease package that created a win-win for both the team and the state. We also had to have the city of New Orleans put its money where its mouth was and commit some land and dollars toward building a practice facility.

And it almost goes without saying, we leaned hard on our business community to secure pledges to purchase the requisite number of season tickets. We far surpassed the very steep requirements, thanks in part to the collaboration of political communities that bought in to our all-out assault. The vast majority of local city politicians were Democrats, while nearly all of the suburban politicians and the governor were Republican.

Tim Coulon, president of suburban Jefferson Parrish, was an incredible ally and partner in this effort and many others. Though he was a Republican and I was a Democrat, we worked together in this and many other joint undertakings to secure many victories for the region.

Governor Mike Foster, a former Democrat turned Republican, and I served together in the Louisiana Senate and had been on fishing trips together when we both served in that body. Foster's chief of staff, Steve Perry, became essential to our efforts in getting the governor and the administration squarely behind our efforts. Bill Hines, a managing partner of the city's largest law firm and a business council leader, accepted my challenge to mobilize the business community in support of our efforts. It was an example of a remarkable, multifaceted Gumbo Coalition that snatched the NBA from Charlotte and brought it to the Big Easy.

We were able to put our ideological differences aside to work for something we all saw as the common good: possession of an NBA franchise and all that such status could potentially bring to our fair city and state.

And, of course, the incomparable Doug Thornton played a huge part in the orchestration of this multifaceted coalition. It was a beautiful thing to see so many diverse individuals representing so many diverse interests and constituencies working side by side to show the NBA brass and the world that a small market could be a successful and worthy NBA home. And we were successful on all fronts. We brought the team to New Orleans, where they play to this day as the New Orleans Pelicans. Our persistence and commitment to community mobilization paid off big-time.

And the payoff was not only immediate. The team has been the gift that keeps on giving. We who made up this NBA franchise-seeking Gumbo Coalition thought that, if we succeeded in our efforts, the NBA would choose our city to host another jewel of a national event—the NBA All-Star Weekend. We figured, as a new NBA city, we would be doing well to host it maybe once every fifteen to twenty years. Since we brought the team to our city, New Orleans has hosted two NBA All-Star Weekend extravaganzas in fifteen years.

Though rejected and momentarily dejected, when another opportunity arose, we didn't wallow in past defeats. Rather, we learned from them and took our shot, going for broke. All this happened in my last months as mayor. So bringing the NBA back to New Orleans, my personal dream, ended up being my parting gift to the city. That gift showed New Orleans' ability to compete with other southern cities vying to attract major corporations. So, in that sense, it was a huge win. And luring a transitioning NBA franchise was no small matter. NBA teams seeking new homes are an extreme rarity. In fact, during the time of our attempts to lure the NBA back to New Orleans, there hadn't been any franchise moves in the NFL or MLB for two decades. For New Orleans to be a chosen and preferred landing spot for one of those rare teams was a huge feather in the city's cap. And to be able to achieve this after striking out with the Timberwolves, being politely thrown out of Commissioner Stern's office, and losing out on the Vancouver Grizzlies, amid Stern's skepticism, amid our small-market status, and amid our underdog persona just made the win all the more sweet.

Three years after this success, Hurricane Katrina hit, and the team had to play in other cities, mainly Oklahoma City, for an entire season. Oklahoma City lobbied for the team to relocate, but our city wasn't having that. The NBA owners sold the team to the NBA, and local billionaire Tom Benson and family purchased the team. And as I said, the team was in jeopardy of leaving after Katrina, but the city rallied around its NBA franchise to keep them in the Big Easy.

Katrina almost caused another professional sports franchise to move, the New Orleans Saints, also owned by the Benson family. And again, it was persistence that proved to be the winning ingredient in holding onto it.

The beloved New Orleans Saints spent their post-Katrina season mainly in San Antonio, Texas, practicing and playing home games. With New Orleans devasted, San Antonio rolling out the welcome wagon, and hard-core recruitment by San Antonio and forces outside that city, the Saints were way closer to being a former New Orleans franchise than most realize.

Though I was no longer mayor of New Orleans, I was still involved in efforts to retain the Saints while president of the NUL.

How? The NFL commissioner, Paul Tagliabue, called me and said Benson was thinking of moving the Saints to San Antonio. I responded, "That's a F'd-up idea." The commissioner said, "That's why I called you, because I need your help."

What he needed was help coalition building. And again, since I was no longer mayor, it wouldn't have been a good look for me or for the current mayor if I was out front in the media waging a campaign to keep the Saints in New Orleans. So I worked behind the scenes, wanting to make sure my moves weren't politicized.

I had worked with Tagliabue before while I was mayor, when, in the wake of 9/11 we could have lost the Super Bowl. The season's entire postseason schedule shifted in the wake of that horrific national tragedy. Though the Super Bowl was scheduled for New Orleans, the change of date meant we had to figure out how to deal with a paying customer who had already booked and paid for that space—a major automotive convention. Amazingly, we were able to move that convention to a week earlier, even though they had already paid for their space, and we were able to keep the Super Bowl from being moved to another city. The coalition building and persistence needed to pull that off must have caught Tagliabue's eye, because as soon as he got word of Benson's plans to move the Saints, he contacted me immediately.

Now, on the NBA deal, I was the quarterback, out front leading and calling plays and audibles when necessary, lining up my offense to be in the best possible position to score. During this Saints/Katrina situation I had to play a supportive role. I was more of a blocking back, the one who clears the way for others to score touchdowns and get all the glory while contributing to the team's success in almost complete anonymity.

I basically called civic and community leaders to tell them that the Saints could leave and that they had to tell them how important they were to the city and that they couldn't leave. I was prepared to play the heavy if I had to and go public with the message that, after the city supported the Saints for generations, it's unjust and immoral for the team to even consider leaving the city due to broken levees and political negligence. I could have easily said this publicly as a former mayor and as head of a civil rights organization, but I kept that tool in my belt.

Instead, others and I worked to assist Benson in selling more season tickets and shoring up other measures of tangible support to make it nearly impossible for him to take the Saints with him to Texas. Our quiet, behind-the-scenes persistence, so different from our NBA strategy, was successful. I can still remember being in the Superdome. It was September 25, 2006, a Monday Night Football game against our rivals, the hated Atlanta Falcons. Just ninety seconds into the game, Saints player Steve Gleason burst up the middle of the Falcons' line and blocked a punt. The ball was sent backwards into the end zone, where Gleason's teammate Curtis Deloatch fell on the ball for a touchdown, giving the hometown team a lead they would never relinquish. They won that night, 23–3. Just three short years later, the Saints, lovable losers of the NFL for decades, won the Super Bowl.

When I reflect on the power of persistence, I can get kind of emotional because I know just how powerful an impact our persistence to attract the Pelicans and keep the Saints has had on the psyche of New Orleanians. Geaux Saints!

GUMBO RECAP: PERSISTENCE VS. PIGHEADEDNESS

A leader knows when to continue the fight and when to abandon a plan and change course. Persistence is having the willingness, ability, and grit to plug away until you attain your goal or realize that your investment of energy would be better spent on some other venture.

Making Persistence Pay Off

Persistence is not blind. It requires a reality check to make sure that the goal is important and attainable.

Persistence demands that you learn from your own efforts in a very honest way, asking yourself, "Why didn't things work the first time(s)?"

Persistence requires that you get out of your own zone and solicit the opinions of others. Their feedback, coming from a different and sometimes objective perspective, can prove invaluable in determining if staying the course, slightly altering the course, or changing the course and destination altogether is the right move.

Persistence beats frustration every time. When you give into frustration, it limits your vision and energy and, hence, limits your opportunities. A mind-set of persistence, even if it leads you to decide to give up and go a different route, is invaluable.

CHAPTER 10

INNOVATION REQUIRES SEEING NEW PATHS

A LEADER MUST SEEK NEW WAYS TO SOLVE OLD PROBLEMS

As the leader of the National Urban League, I recognized that our organization had a long-standing relationship with corporate America and played an extremely significant role in helping overqualified and highly talented African Americans secure employment and careers in all manner of major industries, *Fortune 500* and otherwise. The National Urban League's former CEO, Vernon Jordan, was in fact one of the first black corporate board members in the country, serving on the boards of Xerox and American Express, among others.

Jordan was followed by both John Jacob and Hugh Price, my predecessors, who continued the tradition of serving as corporate board members while they were president and CEO of the National Urban League. No civil rights organization in American history has opened more doors to American corporations for African Americans from entry-level jobs to C-suite and board-level positions than the National Urban League. This is neither brag nor hyperbole, just fact.

The National Urban League has a formidable track record of fighting for racial and gender equality, as well as for the rights of all individuals regardless of race, gender, age, place of origin, religious affiliation, sexual preference, physical ability status, and so on. Over the years, this level of advocacy took many forms, most involving conversations with corporate representatives and elected officials using persuasion, jawboning, public pressure, and more in an effort to change both minds and laws. In other words, we often relied upon handshakes and verbal agreements.

Still, though progress came, it came slowly and without a system for continuing to grow and improve. There were hires here and there, diversity positions created now and again, diversity improvement initiatives started periodically—or, more often, sporadically. The corporations with which we had worked talked about diversity and inclusion as a business imperative, but they didn't treat it as a business imperative. And as an institution committed to advocating for such change, we had to ask ourselves the hard question: "Is our method of advocacy lacking?" The answer: yes.

Too often, our advocacy would result in the sporadic gains already mentioned. But these gains lacked systems and structures to ensure certain things like continued growth and personal accountability for corporations. Thus what we saw when we looked long and hard at the corporations with which we had worked were diversity programs that were more often than not catch-as-catch-can systems, that is, no systems at all. Many treated it as a compliance issue only, trying to avoid legal liability. Moreover, it is axiomatic that all diversity and inclusion efforts arise from the 1964 Civil Rights bill which banned discrimination in employment.

This is by no means to disparage the Herculean work of the NUL and other civil rights and diversity advocates over the decades. Rather, it is to look hard at our mode of operation to look for ways to be more effective at our foundational tasks. This is also not to disparage the companies and corporations with which we have worked in the past, who made good-faith efforts to address blind spots we pointed out in their business models and hiring practices. But it is to say, we can and must all do better.

So how did we approach this old problem in a new, innovative way? It wasn't rocket science, but it was a new approach—one I contend has yielded powerful national benefits.

In 2009, when Comcast announced their intent to purchase NBC Universal, we and the Latino civil rights organization UnidosUS, along with the National Action Network and the NAACP, among others, decided on a different approach. We communicated with Comcast that, for our organizations and constituents to support their deal, we wanted diversity commitments in writing, memorialized as the first memorandum of understanding (MOU) between a multicultural group of organizations and a major corporation.

Essentially, our MOU committed the company to a comprehensive, written strategic plan with goals, timetables, and metrics to measure progress toward diversity. Areas covered include governance, which includes the company's board; personnel, which includes the company's C-suite; procurement, which includes the company's spending on goods and services and philanthropy and community investment. The plan also included a commitment for Comcast to carry new channels owned by people of color, channels selected through a competitive process.

Though it seemed a small tweak in our approach, the move had a formidable impact. Comcast, with its executive vice president, David Cohen, in the lead, committed to producing the company's first diversity plan and forty-member diversity advisory council. In addition, Comcast committed to increasing the level of diversity on its corporate board, in its lauded philanthropic efforts, in its hiring practices, in its programming efforts, and in its supply chain.

The agreement wasn't perfect, but its purpose to make measurable progress has been achieved, and it has systems in place to keep the progress moving forward and benchmarks to see what's working and what's not. The company also committed to convene twice a year to provide updates on their diversity plan's progress.

This MOU was not created to cut deals for individuals but rather to ensure fairness from a company whose customer base was and is only growing more diverse. And this approach has proven to be incredibly more effective than the handshakes and verbal commitments. With goals on paper and committed to and with regular update meetings scheduled, a system, albeit not perfect, has been implemented, and it's been used since to facilitate change. It was a small change, yet it was a new approach to an old problem. It was an innovation that continues to pay dividends.

For one perspective, Comcast is a global media and technology company with two primary businesses: Comcast Cable and NBCUniversal. Comcast Cable is one of the United States' largest video, high-speed Internet, and phone providers (under the XFINITY brand).

Additionally, Comcast provides security and automation services and wireless cell phone service under the brand Xfinity Mobile. The company has twenty-nine million customer relationships in the United States (thirty-nine states and Washington, DC). In other words, they're everywhere.

The other part of this behemoth is NBCUniversal, one of the world's leading media and entertainment companies and owner of too many entities to name. But to show you how embedded they are in black and brown communities, and vice versa, I'll name a few: NBC, Telemundo, NBC News, CNBC, MSNBC, NBC Sports, USA Network, E!, Bravo, Syfy, Universal Pictures, Focus Features, Illumination Entertainment, DreamWorks Animation, Universal Cable Productions, Telemundo Studios, and Universal Television. They also own two leading television station groups, renowned theme parks in the United States, Japan, and Singapore, and scores of Internet-based businesses.

My point: this is not a mom-and-pop entity but a *Fortune 50* company we have an MOU with to help hold them accountable to diversity goals that benefit not only our communities but the company's bottom line. And Comcast is not the only one.

When AT&T bought DirecTV, they provided our Gumbo Coalition of civil rights organizations a commitment letter; it wasn't as strong as an MOU, but it was something that operates on the same principle.

In 2016, we reached a third agreement with Charter Communications, an agreement made with a multicultural group of twelve organizations. Charter committed to create and implement a diversity plan, a diversity council, and frameworks for not only holding themselves accountable but for recognizing the role of the twelve organizations in holding them accountable.

This different approach, which moves beyond verbal agreements, creates goals and a framework by which Charter's diversity can be measured, and it creates an active board and committee made up of a broad array of constituents, including people of color to advise them in their efforts.

With Charter, we are three to four years into the MOU agreement. Before the MOU, Charter did not have a chief diversity officer or a diversity plan. Now they do. Before these MOUs, it was as I said before, "catch-as-catch-can." These agreements put these corporations in partnership with these civil rights organizations.

Interestingly, I was told that Charter CEO Tom Rutledge was not inclined to agree to an MOU before his scheduled meeting with me and Rev. Al Sharpton. To open the meeting, we told him we wanted to help him build a great company, and for that to be, the company had to be diverse. His response was, "What do I have to do?" We told him Charter had to partner with us in all the ways that I mentioned above. Immediately, he said, "Sounds great. What do I need to do?" He completely surprised us with his willingness to get on board.

Our approach with Rutledge was the same as it has been with other CEOs: to convince him that the MOU approach is better than an ad hoc, piecemeal approach, and that these MOUs are not perfect, but are better than anything else.

Charter Communications is the second largest telecommunications and mass media company in the United States. It's a behemoth by any standard, serving over twenty-nine million customers in over forty-one states. As a cable operator, Charter Communications is second only to Comcast.

Charter responded to our MOU by creating a position of chief diversity officer and an Office of Diversity and Inclusion. They added three people of color to their board, took steps to increase hiring people of color, and started increasing diversity in their supplier chain. And you have to remember, this monumental company had no infrastructure, no plan for doing this before our agreed-upon MOU.

And these deals were not only good for the businesses; they have been good for customers, citizens in general, and children impacted by the daily images they see on TV and online. Think about it, Lester Holt is now anchoring the evening news on NBC. On some mornings you can turn on *The Today Show*, and three of the four hosts are African American. This quiet but powerful explosion of diversity happened post-MOU.

Comcast is going to hit almost $3 billion doing business with minority suppliers. Before their MOU, they weren't even at $1 billion.

Another important thing to note is these MOUs were drafted when these companies were buying another company and needed government approval, which meant they needed our support and endorsement. And these are companies that sell to the masses—to tens of millions of people—and Sean Combs, Magic Johnson, TV One would not have channels to reach these viewers without these MOUs. And the same could be said for the Latino channels created post-MOUs. In other words, the MOU mandated the founding of these channels.

As a news junkie, one of the many channels I watch religiously is MSNBC. If you look at MSNBC on any given evening, you see an array of black commentators that were not there before 2008. The numbers have shot up dramatically. And when you pair that with the reality that "a picture is worth a thousand words," think about how this visible diversity has impacted and continues to impact young minds and old. We know the increase has been dramatic not simply by using the eyeball test but because the MOU requires tracking this information.

Simply put, these MOUs, a new solution to an old problem, advance diversity in ways the old methods did not and could not. I suggested to Facebook and Google that they should take the same approach as a way to address the dearth of black and brown workers as documented in the 2018 *State of Black America* report, "Powering the Digital Revolution."

The report found that, in 2014, of the almost forty thousand employees of the four major tech firms, fewer than one thousand were African American.

To be fair, Facebook has begun to take some steps, which include conducting a civil rights audit led by the highly respected civil rights advocate Laura Murphy. Facebook has also added to its board the highly respected Ken Chenault, the former CEO of American Express.

Google's parent company, Alphabet Inc., followed suit by adding Roger Ferguson, chairman of TIAA and a former Federal Reserve Bank governor, to its board as their first African American member.

Now, some people aren't as bullish on these MOUs as I am. In fact, there are those whom I would classify as downright haters. They contend these MOUs haven't done much of anything. But let me tell you what these MOUs did do. Did I mention the channels owned by Sean Combs and Magic Johnson? Did I mention the diversity explosion on MSNBC and other major stations? Did I mention these *Fortune 50* companies—not *Fortune 500*, but *Fortune 50*—have raised by billions of dollars how much they have bought from diversity suppliers, or in other words, underrepresented minority and women-owned businesses? Did I mention systems put in place to increase the diversity in hiring, increase the diversity of those on the leadership track and in the supply chain, and other programs instituted to expand diversity? Yes, I did. But they are worth repeating.

Truth be told, we haven't achieved in senior executive positions. Forget a glass ceiling, there are titanium ceilings that don't want to give an inch. But orderly, trackable progress has been made. I pioneered this approach, chartered it, and led it to provide African American, Latino, Asian, LGBTQ, and disability leaders and groups access to a seat at the table. In fact, the aforementioned diversity breakdown aptly describes Charter's diversity council members.

Tom Rutledge, David Cohen, and Randall Stephenson are not only *Fortune 100* corporate executives, they are living, breathing witnesses to the value of establishing MOU partnerships as opposed to relying on nothing but verbal promises and handshakes.

This doesn't mean there is no more employment discrimination, or that these MOUs are a silver bullet, or that we are past the need for aggressive, external activism. But it's better than the ad hoc approach that favors begging one minute and idle threats the next. It's an approach that requires intelligence and pressure, and some goodwill from the companies. For me, this is a legacy that will long outlive me.

GUMBO RECAP: FINDING THE INNOVATION ADVANTAGE

Not all innovations involve new technology. This may seem like a crazy assertion in a world dominated by AI advancements and new generations of tech products replacing the "old products" at an exponential rate. Computers and apps and social media platforms have become so foundational to our twenty-first-century way of life that it is hard for many to picture life without them. Leaders, however, can find opportunities for innovation almost anywhere—in new tech products or merely new ideas and approaches.

Identifying Ways and Means to Allow Innovation to Work for You

As with all things, honesty is critical for identifying avenues for innovation. Innovation, at its core, is about applying new solutions to

HarperCollinsPublishers

old problems. This means having to be honest with the result you are currently achieving and painstakingly reevaluating your go-to approach(es).

Innovation requires a lifelong learning mind-set. This means you are always reading about and researching what others are doing to facilitate transformational growth and change. This means being a student of others in your industry while also being a curious learner willing to venture into new vistas. New vistas may provide new ideas.

Multiple businesses and individuals have adopted the mantra "Fail fast." In a society that abhors "failure," the value of these words may be hard to discern. But the lesson here is, be willing to try new things instead of studying them for five months to five years. The quicker you are willing to try new and creative ways and approaches, the sooner you will find what works for you. This will also mean you may quickly find what doesn't work for you. But that's okay. In fact, that's the point. Finding out what doesn't work is invaluable information for directing you to processes and approaches that do.

CHAPTER 11

NOW WE GOT GUMBO

As a forty-plus-year veteran of public speaking on a wide range of topics, most on the topic of leadership, I have become fairly proficient at being able to share hard truths in a language palatable for my audience. Well, here's a hard truth for you. Most people are diversity averse.

Few of us readily admit this. Fewer still are proud of it, but it's true. It has to be. How else can you explain why most of us live in communities surrounded by neighbors who look and think like us? Most of us attended schools with classmates and teachers who look and think like us. Most of us attend houses of faith filled predominantly with worshippers who look and think like us. Most of us work with, hire, and do business with professionals who look and think like us. No matter how much we say we value diversity or use diverse stock photos in our organizational literature or quote diversity catchphrases, our actions state that we, like most people, are diversity averse.

We operate in this diversity-wary space in spite of the mountainous research that shows companies, schools, and other organizations that are more diverse in terms of race, gender, faith, sexual preference, and sociopolitical perspectives far outpace their competition in terms of profits, market share, and overall effectiveness. Regardless of which metric they use, they all come back with the same response: diversity is excellent for the bottom line. Yet our societal hard truth persists.

I was moved to write *The Gumbo Coalition* because I believe in the power and importance of leadership. I also believe in the efficacy of diversity and coalition building, especially how they play themselves out in the health and success of organizations. This diversity-focused, Gumbo Coalition leadership paradigm has served me well over the decades, as an attorney, state legislator, mayor, and president of a national nonprofit. I believe it can also serve the entire nation.

When giving one of my many addresses, I often refer to one particular story, or rather, historical example, that highlights the importance of leadership and diversity. It has been so universally well received by people of all socioeconomic, educational, and political stripes that I thought I might offer it here to make my case for a national Gumbo Coalition movement.

In one of the most pivotal and defining moments in American history, it was leaders who championed diversity and coalition building that made all the difference in the world.

Between the late 1880s and the early 1920s, this country experienced an unprecedented wave of immigrants arriving on these shores. The vast majority were Irish and Italian. In other words, they were Catholics, coming to America when Catholics were not very welcome.

Paralleling this wave of immigration was the beginning of the Great Migration—that migration through which millions of blacks fled cotton, sugar cane, and tobacco economies of the South as mechanization, the destruction of crops brought by the boll weevil, the Ku Klux Klan, and the backlash toward Reconstruction forced many blacks to travel to the cities of the Northeast and Midwest. It was in these circumstances and against this backdrop that the National Urban League was formed.

There was also a large contingent of immigrants coming from Eastern Europe. These were mainly Jews, another group that felt the cold shoulder of the majority of America's citizenry. What many history books gloss over is that, during this period in our nation's story, there was a national movement afoot to guard against the "immigrant problem."

These new arrivals were declared by an embarrassingly large number of people to be lazy, criminal, and destroyers of the fabric of the country. "Something needs to be done about this immigrant problem before they overrun the country and change the complexion and basic makeup of America," many shouted.

They called for swift and decisive actions on this "problem," because America was still vying to become a global player. It's hard for us to wrap our twenty-first-century minds around the fact that America was not always the global power it is today. But during that period, many countries, mostly in Europe, were jockeying for that position. And to some, this flood of immigrants to the United States meant confusion regarding what it meant to be an American. This posed, for some, a threat to the nation's chances at global leadership.

An internal, national clash seemed imminent.

Even amid the brewing national animosity and discord, some leaders looked at the new Americans and saw in them the labor force that was needed to drive the industrial revolution. So leaders, if you will, formed coalitions with these immigrants and migrants, putting them to work en masse. And these workers became the engine that helped drive America to emerge as a global force.

To be certain, African American migrants faced employment and housing discrimination of untold measures. But America's twentieth-century manufacturing revolution would not have succeeded without black workers in the steel, rubber, glass, and automobile manufacturing plants of the Northeast and Midwest.

And when wars arose that threatened the American way of life, many of these immigrants, along with the tens of thousands of forced migrants—children of formerly enslaved Africans—made up a huge portion of the soldiers who won world wars and set America on a path of unprecedented global dominance as the world's preeminent superpower.

History does not fully honor those business and labor leaders who worked behind the scenes to open America's industrial revolution to a more diverse workforce. Certainly, their work was not as personally dangerous and life threatening as the work of the tens of thousands of named and unnamed Civil Rights Movement participants. In my opinion, these civil rights workers have yet to receive their full due for the incredible service they rendered to this country and the world as they stood for freedom and equality. Those who made inspiring public speeches and those who made bold displays of courage as foot soldiers, marching and protesting and sitting in and standing up, had tremendous impact on the opening of those doors to employment.

But those courageous, frontline business and labor leaders, who did their part to open up new vistas for those so long shut out of the American Dream, deserve their story told as well.

Amazingly, because individuals willingly displayed true leadership, even though discrimination was palpable and obvious, the nation became a global superpower thanks to this rainbow coalition of Civil Rights Movement workers doing their part and business and labor leaders doing theirs by helping white immigrants and black migrants become the workforce behind this transformation.

Often, the past can teach us powerful lessons about what we need to do now and how we can move into the future. This is one of those times.

What those late-nineteenth- and early-twentieth-century immigrants and migrants added to this nation had incalculable impact—

all because their energy, efforts, and ingenuity were brought into the mix. Transformational leaders facilitated the building of coalitions that brought these different individuals and communities together. The result: growing industries at home and respected leadership and influence abroad.

Now, what does all this have to do with the Gumbo Coalition? I'm glad you asked.

As the head of your school, business, or organization, you can become more efficient, more effective, and more impactful by championing diversity and coalition building. And even though you may operate at a local level, there is no telling how great or how far your openness to diversity and coalition building will reverberate.

Think about it. Those 1890s business owners could not have foreseen the challenges of world wars this nation would face. But because they were open to diversity, even if for selfish, personal business reasons, they opened the door to more Americans being able to share their gifts and lend their talents, muscle, and ingenuity to America's cause.

Remarkably, our nation finds itself at another global crossroads, with China, India, and others vying for the leader's chair. America has been able to maintain its position because, though we have our diversity-averse inclinations, we've allowed for diversity and coalition building to flourish in pockets here and pockets there, just enough for us to hold onto the role as the greatest global influencer.

Just imagine what would happen if we were to make inclusion and diversity the norm rather than the exception. Companies and schools and organizations with leaders who have already embraced this Gumbo Coalition model are enjoying the benefits of their labor.

The tools provided in this book are more than enough to equip you to be that kind of twenty-first- and twenty-second-century leader who will shake up the world and inspire others to follow. And hey, isn't that what leadership is? Using your gifts to inspire others to follow?

The Gumbo Coalition we built in New Orleans was both powerful and special. I contend the time is right to expand upon that work for the good of the entire country. America needs a national Gumbo Coalition movement right now because the ingredients for the most diverse gumbo in the world are already at our fingertips. This nation is becoming more diverse not just by the day, but by the hour and even the minute. We have all the spices and flavors needed to create all manner of coalitions. You have all the ingredients you need to create new partnerships and collaborations and be a standout leader in your field while also serving as a guidepost of other leaders, both in your field and beyond.

Gumbo Coalition leadership means you're willing to strategize and put plans together in consensus and collaboration with others, rather than letting different entities or departments work in silos. Gumbo Coalition leaders welcome the idea of working on parallel and integrated tracks that overflow with diverse views and skills. Such leaders know their results will be far superior because they are drawing from a deeper well of knowledge and experiences.

Gumbo Coalition leadership is about amassing power and influence and using them to bring others on board or warn them to get out of the way.

Gumbo Coalition leadership puts in the work to learn as much as humanly possible about as many individuals, movements, departments, and innovations as possible, because people who possess intellectual curiosity are often open to diversity and coalition building.

Remember when, earlier in the book, I shared the story of watching the late-night public-access broadcasts of the city council meetings? If you recall, a police department representative's comment about having overtime money to spare gave me the idea of where to find the money to bolster youth programs.

Watching those late-night broadcasts was not in my job description. No one in the entire city would have faulted me for not tuning in. It was simply my intellectual curiosity and desire to gather as much information as possible to help me as mayor. That was an example of Gumbo Coalition leadership, and at its essence, it is no different than the leader who actively seeks to build coalitions to strengthen the likelihood of success.

The late Dr. Susan J. Herman—a professor of management at the University of Alaska, Fairbanks, professor emerita of management at Keene State College, and founder of multiple iconic leadership development programs for youth in Fairbanks—broke down leadership into three parts. All three speak to the value of Gumbo Coalition leadership:

"I define leadership as having three parts: First is seeing what needs to be done to make things better or seeing a problem that needs fixing. Second is having the vision, the skill, and the wherewithal to change the system. And third is the most important task of mobilizing the energy of others to organize and act in ways to achieve that vision."[1]

I agree with Dr. Herman's assessment wholeheartedly. Gumbo Coalition leadership is willing to see what needs to be done, to look squarely at the challenges to formulate next steps.

Gumbo Coalition leadership is about having or amassing the vision, skills, and wherewithal to meet challenges with solutions and opportunities. This screams of coalition building and the need to be open to diversity.

Former NBA player and legendary coach Pat Riley often repeated the words written by Max DePree in his book *Leadership Is an Art*: "The first responsibility of a *leader* is to *define reality*." Those business leaders of the late-nineteenth and early-twentieth centuries defined reality when they boldly chose diversity and coalition building over divisiveness and exclusion. But, lo and behold, they not only defined reality, they helped shape a new reality for this country for decades, even generations, to come—all because they in their time were open to practicing Gumbo Coalition leadership.

By taking advantage of the ten leadership lessons of this book, you will not only be a better leader for those in your orbit, you may very well be setting the pace for a new century of global influence for the country. So now that you have the recipe, get in the kitchen and get to cooking. And please remember, gumbo is not a solitary dish. It was created to be shared—literally.

And the beautiful thing about gumbo, besides its fantastic taste and the warm way it makes you feel, is that it's a dish that always welcomes new additions. Imagine a business, a school, a civic organization, a nonprofit that operated in such a manner—open to new people with new and different ideas, each bringing a different spice and flavor to the dish. With each passing day, I am more confirmed in my belief in diversity, my belief in coalition building, my belief in leadership that can galvanize and bring these powers out of those in their charge. When this happens for you, and it can, you already know what I'll say: "Now we got gumbo."

Afterword

As a leader on the hardwood and in the executive suite, I have received numerous accolades for being able to commune the talents, passions, and energies of diverse people for a common cause. I have also been acknowledged for successfully bringing seemingly unrelated entities together to work in coalition for the benefit of all involved. That said, *The Gumbo Coalition* offers a priceless gift to the readers as it speaks to leadership in a refreshing new way. What I loved about *The Gumbo Coalition* is that it celebrates the idea of lifelong learning with a purpose. It recognizes that there is no such thing as "arriving" as a leader. Marc Morial and this phenomenal book recognize that we are all works in progress.

Marc and I have a very special connection. First, because his twin passions mirror my own—leadership and diversity. Second, because of what he has done for both.

I've known Marc for many years, and I have seen him in action making things happen. But nothing told me more about the power of his leadership skills than Marc's ability to lead the charge to bring the National Basketball Association (NBA) back to the Big Easy. The city of New Orleans had two runs with professional basketball franchises, one in the American Basketball Association and the other in the NBA. Both teams ended up leaving town, and the second time on not-so-good terms with the NBA's league office. So, in the minds of many, it was a mission impossible to think the NBA would ever venture back into New Orleans. In my opinion, one of the only persons who could have successfully brought back professional basketball to New Orleans was the then-second-term mayor of the city, Marc Morial. Marc had the leadership acumen to build a coalition diverse and dynamic enough to achieve the unachievable. In 2002, the New Orleans Hornets made their season debut.

In *The Gumbo Coalition*, Marc doesn't treat diversity as just a buzzword or a bothersome hurdle as many companies or leaders begrudgingly do. Rather, Marc exalts diversity (gumbo) as a source of great strength, growth potential, and dynamic innovations—and as an imperative for leaders to embrace and actively cultivate if they want to achieve success.

There are four consistent themes that find their way in each chapter that I believe are key: 1) cultivating a seeker's heart; 2) recognizing the power of relationships; 3) possessing a willingness to be fluid; and 4) having the courage to be steadfast and unmovable.

A seeker is always looking for ways to improve and approaches learning as a joyous daily task. *The Gumbo Coalition*'s words of wisdom reveal just how important possessing a seeker's attitude is to be an effective leader.

Also important to a leader's strength is relationships, a concept not often highlighted in leadership or business-related works. However, it is apparent throughout Marc's life and throughout the chapters of this book that cultivating and nurturing multiple levels of relationships is a "secret roux" many would do well to add to their gumbo.

The final two themes that really spoke to me are: 1) being fluid—being able to move, change, and adjust to new realities; and 2) being steadfast—as there are some things for which a leader, no matter how fluid they may be, must be unmovable. A leader's values, level of integrity, and work ethic are rocks upon which a leader cannot be stirred. *The Gumbo Coalition* reveals both of these critical skills—the ability to adjust on the fly when necessary while also being unwavering in one's vision and values, no matter the issues you face.

One of my challenges to the readers of this book is to incorporate these themes in your everyday. Marc uses storytelling as one of his teaching techniques. The most effective learning takes place when it becomes personal. Use the principles and lessons from *The Gumbo Coalition* to lead with purpose, network with intention, and to spread the word about the effectiveness of building diverse coalitions that will aid in the betterment of the world we all live in.

—Earvin "Magic" Johnson

Notes

SECTION ONE

1. According to the November 6, 2007, article "New Orleans murder rate for year will set record" by Ethan Brown (www.theguardian.com), "During the mid-1990s New Orleans reigned as the nation's murder capital, a frenzy of violence and drug dealing fomented in part by a police force that had grown almost irredeemably corrupt. Indeed, in 1994 federal prosecutors indicted 10 New Orleans cops on drug trafficking charges. More dramatically, that same year a New Orleans officer named Len Davis was charged with ordering the murder of a woman who had filed a police brutality complaint against him."

SECTION TWO

1. According to the April 18, 2018, article "Acceptance of LGBT people and rights has increased around the world," found at williamsinstitute.law.ucla.edu, "New research from the Williams Institute at UCLA School of Law finds average levels of acceptance for LGBT people and rights have increased globally since 1980, though acceptance has become more polarized, increasing in the most accepting countries and decreasing in the least." In addition, according to GLAAD's annual TV diversity report, LGBTQ representation on TV hit a record high in 2018 (https://www.theverge.com/2018/10/26/18028908/glaad-report-television-tv-2018-lgbtq-diversity-gay-bisexual-trans-media-representation).

2. Several articles connect the HIV / AIDS epidemic with rising levels of violence against LGBTQ individuals. One article found in the *Journal of Social Aspects of HIV/AIDS* (https: / / www.ncbi.nlm.nih.gov / pmc / articles / PMC6060376 /) focuses on this reality in South Africa. The November 15, 2004, article "Hated to Death" examined this topic from the context of Jamaica's growing HIV / AIDS epidemic (https: / / www.hrw.org / report / 2004 / 11 / 15 / hated-death / homophobia-violence-and-jamaicas-hiv / aids-epidemic).
3. Representative Davis's comment on "nigger blood" was reported in the *New York Times*. It was also used as an example of racism in the *Multi Ethnic Handbook, Vol. 1*, that was prepared by the Michigan Education Association's Division of Minority Affairs (1973). The publication contained "Lesson Plans for Teaching Concepts Dealing with Racism Contributions of Blacks, Latinos, Native Americans." (https: / / files.eric.ed.gov / fulltext / ED115724.pdf).

CHAPTER FOUR

1. http: / / theneworleanstribune.com / 2017 / 05 / 09 / lsu-names-building-on-campus -in-honor-of-new-orleans-native-clarence-barney-jr / .
2. Most sources, including "Governor: Evac Superdome, Rescue Centers," Fox News, and Associated Press (August 30, 2005), report between fifteen and twenty thousand people populated the Louisiana Superdome during Hurricane Katrina, though a few sources, including the article "From Despair to Hope: How One National Guardswoman Reconciles Memories of Katrina," place that number between thirty and thirty-five thousand (http: / / www.espn .com / espnw / features / article / 13514606 / hurricane-katrina-superdome-new -orleans-national-guard).
3. "Hurricane Katrina, explained" by Sarah Gibbens, January 16, 2019 (https: / / www.nationalgeographic.com / environment / natural-disasters / reference / hurricane-katrina /). Another source, "Hurricane Katrina: Facts, Damage & Aftermath," by Kim Ann Zimmerman (August 27, 2015), reported that 1,833 people died during Hurricane Katrina (https: / / www.livescience.com / 22522 -hurricane-katrina-facts.html).
4. Gibbens, "Hurricane Katrina, explained."
5. Gibbens, "Hurricane Katrina, explained."

CHAPTER FIVE

1. While delivering remarks at the US Conference of Mayors' meeting on October 25, 2001, in Washington, DC, Morial referenced the work of the meeting referenced above (https: / / www.c-span.org / video / ?166917-2 / emergency-safety -security-summit).

CHAPTER SIX

1. The NRA's response to the lawsuit filed by Morial is discussed in the *Frontline* (PBS) article "Inside the 'Other' Gun Lobby" by Sarah Childress, February 19, 2013 (https://www.pbs.org/wgbh/frontline/article/inside-the-other-gun-lobby/).

CHAPTER NINE

1. On May 24, 1994, the *Los Angeles Times* reported that the Minnesota Timberwolves were relocating to New Orleans contingent upon the Timberwolves' owners, Harvey Ratner and Marv Wolfenson, receiving a payment of $152.5 million for the team from the ownership group of Top Rank (https://www.latimes.com/archives/la-xpm-1994-05-24-sp-61540-story.html). According to an August 6, 1994, post on postbulletin.com, the Top Rank deal was spearheaded by boxing promoter Bob Arum.

CHAPTER ELEVEN

1. The quote by Dr. Herman was found at https://www.feminist.com/resources/quotes/leadership.htm, as referenced by noted author Elaine Berstein Partnow, whose works focus on Jewish women in leadership.

Index

ABOUT THE AUTHOR

MARC MORIAL is the former second-generation New Orleans mayor who oversaw many improvements during his terms, including crime reduction, police reform, and the passing of a significant bond issue. In May 2003, Morial was appointed president and CEO of the National Urban League. Since that appointment, Morial's Empowerment Agenda has worked to reenergize the League's diverse constituencies, build on the strength of its nearly one-hundred-year-old legacy, and increase its profile both locally and nationally.

ABOUT THE EDITOR

LAVAILLE LAVETTE is a bestselling author and editor of numerous books, including *New York Times* bestsellers. With a master's in education, Lavaille has worked as an investment broker, schoolteacher, school district administrator, speechwriter, and marketing executive, and she has served as special advisor to former US secretary of education Rod Paige. Currently, Lavaille is president and publisher of two imprints, One Street Books and Ebony Magazine Publishing, in partnership with HarperCollins Publishers.

Printed in the USA
CPSIA information can be obtained
at www.ICGtesting.com
JSHW030947130923
48374JS00028B/531

9 781400 216314